HISTORY OF MEDIEVAL ANDHRADESA

HISTORY OF MEDIEVAL ANDHRADESA

M. KRISHNA KUMARI

GIAN PUBLISHING HOUSE
NEW DELHI - 110002

HISTORY OF MEDIEVAL ANDHRADESA

ISBN 9788121202671

Reprint in 2017 in India by
Gyan Publishing House
5, Main Ansari Road, Daryaganj,
New Delhi - 110002
Phone: 9811692060

E-mail : books@gyanbooks.com
gyanbook@vsnl.com
Website: gyanbooks.com

Preface

This volume is designed to contain twenty-three papers, on medieval Andhra history from tenth to thirteenth centuries, published earlier in various journals. The aim and scope of the papers along with the organisation of the volume is explained in 'Introduction'. Further, it also includes discussions on the latest trends in recent studies by several historians.

Majority of the eassys of this book are based on epigraphical sources. Some of the papers bring to light, for the first time, either new epigraphical sources, or a fresh survey and new interpretation for the already known sources that are not studied critically so far. The papers based on sculptural and monumental data also bring to light the new evidence of the construction of monuments by the Velanāti Chōḷas and the Eastern Gangas, which have not been dealt with in the past studies. A new approach has been made on studying the images of Bhimesvara temple at Samalkot.

Many eminent scholars in the fields of epigraphy and art have offered their help to me in writing these papers, an outcome of my thirteen years of research work. In this connection, I wish to express my gratitude to Sri N. Sethuraman, Prof. Gift Siromoney, Prof. M.G.S. Narayanan, Dr. M.N. Katti, Dr. S.P. Tewari, Prof. Y. Subbarayalu, Dr. S.S. Ramachandramurty, Dr. P.V. Parabrahma Sastry and Prof. R. Champaka Lakshmi for their valuable suggestions and new ideas in dealing with the subject. I thank my colleagues Prof. C. Somasundara Rao and Prof. K. Sundaram, with whom I had fruitful discussions on various topics.

I thank the editors of the following journals for having published these essays earlier in their journals ; *India Past and Present* (Bombay), *Itihas* (Hyderabad), *Bharati* (Vijayawada), *The journal of The Place Names Society* (*Mysore*),

The Journal of Archaeological Studies, Editorial Boards of *Andhra Pradesh History Congress, South Indian History Congress* and *Indian History Congress.*

I acknowledge the assistance of Sri B.A. Nelson Babu, Smt. K. Jayasree and Smt. J. Vijaya Lakshmi in compilation of this volume with pleasure. Mr. M. Appa Rao, steno-typist deserves appreciation for typing the manuscript.

I fẹel pleasure in presenting this volume, as it is hoped to cater to the needs of students and researchers interested in medieval Andhra History.

M. Krishna Kumari

Introduction

This volume contains twenty-three papers of the author on the various aspects of history and culture of Āndhradēśa of 10th to 13th centuries A. D. The main concern of these studies is to highlight the evidence of the epigraphical sources, which have not been critically studied earlier, and to bring to light the new epigraphical and monumental sources.

The works of eminent scholars, like K.A.N. Sastri, N. Venkataramanayya, Mallampalli Somasekhara Sarma, T.V. Mahalingam and B.V. Krishna Rao, are based upon the foundations of concrete epigraphic evidence. Hence their works remain as the most authoritative political histories of the pre-modern period. Though they have provided the much needed and reliable chronological framework for the study of the history of South India as well as Andhra, the narrative elements cast shadow over the political history. It is treated as a separate domain from the basic social and economic changes. Further the growth in the science and technology as well as cultural progress are treated as ancillary to the political history. Even the recent works on medieval Andhra,[1] falls in the same direction though they fill the gap in the dynastic history. They have treated the subject like the earlier writers i.e., in the compartmental pattern of organisation into political history, administration, socio-economic conditions, religion, literature and art, and so on. However, the American historians like Burton Stein, George Spencer and Kenneth R. Hall, who have concentrated on the South Indian historical studies have set a new trend in South Indian historiography. While their main concern was on Chōḷa-maṇḍalam, they made certain generalisations on Andhra region which was treated as a peripheral zone. These generalisations are based on secondary sources due to the inclusion of a vast period, relating to Chōḷa and Vijayanagara states, for their study. Further, the variety of languages of South India with which they were dealing necessitated them to resort to secondary sources. In their studies, they have used the sociological theories like the 'Peasant Society' and 'Segmentary State,' in which the logic of theory is not correlated properly with the epigraphical evidence. Even though the "plunder politics" theory advanced by George W. Spencer and Kenneth Hall is suggestive, (according to which the Chōḷa state was a powerful predatory organism thriving on large scale plunder, instead of the periodical collection of revenue) it is not adequately supported by the available epigraphical evidence.

The several papers included in this work are solely based on the epigraphical sources material. Considering the limitations of the past studies, the recent trend of using statistical methods has been introduced in the study of the inscriptions. The application of the statistical methods used by Noboru Karashima, Y. Subbarayalu and others[2] in dealing with the Tamil inscriptions relating to socio-economic analysis of history has yielded good results. This kind of study has not been made so far, as regards to a number of Telugu stone inscriptions found on the temple walls. To determine the general tendencies, particulary for socio-economic analysis, one has to gather all the concerned epigraphs and process them statistically. . To rule out ambiguity relating to the socio-economic conditions of any period, statistical analysis of the vast epigraphical data is useful. Hence, in this work, land and village donations made to the temples during the medieval period are statistically analysed.

As it has been stated earlier, the recently published works of Burton Stein and his Amrican followers on South Indian History are based on sociological models and they outrightly rejected the Marxian concept of feudalism.[3] The theory of 'Segmentary State' used by Stein as an alternative model to the "centralised state" theory of the traditional historians has often been questioned.[4] Considering the evidence of the Telugu Stone and Copper plate record of the period, it has been shown in this work that efforts had been made by Kulōttuṅgaī to build up a politically integrated and powerful state during his reign-period by sending several Tamil officers like *Pallavarārayar*, *Brahma mārāvar* and Muvenda Velan of the State. N. Karashima and Stein are reluctant to view the political organisation of the Chōḷa state as based on the concepts of feudalism. Few inscriptions of Drākshārāma critically studied in this work will show that various traits of political feudalism comparable to the feudal society of medieval Europe existed in the medieval polity of Āndhradēśa.

Though studies on political history of medieval Andhra have been made earlier, by scholars like V. Yasoda Devi,[5] K.A.N. Sastri,[6] B.V. Krishna Rao,[7]

M. Somasekhara Sarma[8] and others, they have not considered the historicity of Rājādhirāja of the Drākshārāma inscriptions but inclined to identify him with the reigning Chola rulers, whoever is on the Chōla throne by the dates of the inscriptions. An attempt is made in this volume to present the epigraphical evidence from a different perspective. Also the date of commencement of Rajadhiraja II's rule in Andhra region is thoroughly discussed. The influence of the Tamil people and their culture is profound in Andhra area, particularly in Krishṇā-Gōdāvarī valleys, because of the rule of the Chāḷukya-Chōḷas during the medieval times. While studying the medieval inscriptions of Āndhradēśa, generally one confronts with the problem of the records of Vishnuvardhana *Mahārājas*. All the inscriptions mentioning Vishṇuvardhana *Mahārājas* and the usual eastern Chāḷukyan epithets are collected, arranged and classified in such a manner, to distinguish the Vishṇuvardhana *Mahārājas* of the main royal line with that of the minor ruling Chāḷukyan families.

The sculptural and monumental sources form the other important feature of this volume. In studying the images or sculptures of the temples, so far, the iconographical features of the images extant are compared with the descriptions mentioned in the Śilpa texts. Recently, iconometric studies with the application of computer methods are carried out by Prof. Gift Siromoney and his colleagues on the facial proportions of the sculptures of Kailāsanātha temple of Kāñchipuram and Mahābalipuram, which gave good results.[9] Following the methodology evolved by them, the sculptures of the Chāḷukya Bhīmēsvara temple at Chāḷukya Bhīmavaram (Samalkot), which is renowned as one of the Panchārāma shrines of medieval times have been subjected to the iconometric analysis. This is aimed mainly to see whether, or not, the sculptors of the Chalukyan times have followed the iconometric measurements prescribed in the Śilpa texts. The result shows that there is no significant difference between the canonical measurements and the observed measurements of the images. Further, it also helped in characterising the sculptures of Chāḷukya Bhīma I period in terms of sculptural proportions and to compare them with the images of the remaining *Panchārama* shrines.

Panchānana Śiva of Avanigadda, *Śarabhēsa mūrti* of Drākshārāma and *Harihara pitāmaha* of Valiveru are some of the unnoticed and unpublished images, which are studied and discussed in this volume with the help of iconographical texts. The paper dealing with the architectural details and sculptural wealth of the Eastern Ganga temple of Gallavalli, which has not been studied earlier by the art historians, is also included.

The volume has been divided into two sections. Section-I covers (1 to 8 and 13) the various political aspects of the period including the problems of viceroyalty in the Vēngī region, succession to the Chōḷa throne, the historicity of Rajadhiraja of the Drākshārāma inscriptions, identification of the kings mentioned in the inscriptions, Tamil influence on the personal and place names and language of the lithic records. Besides these essays on political history, the author included essays (10 to 12) relating to the land transactions, personal and communal land-holdings, agrahāra donations, role of the mahājana organisations, state and village donations. Apart from the above, the newly discovered copper plate grant of the eastern Gāṅga king Rājarāja Dēvēndravarma (15) is analysed.

Section-II includes papers (1 to 8) relating to the study of the architectural lineament of the temples of the Velāṇḍu Chōḷas and the Eastern Gāṅgas iconographical studies on the images of the time of the Eastern Chalukyas, Chāḷukya-Chōḷas and the iconometric study of the images of Chāḷukya Bhīmavaram temple at Samalkot.

REFERENCES

1. M. Krishna Kumari, *Rule of the Chāḷukya-Chōḷas in Āndhradēśa*, Delhi, 1985 ; K. Suryanarayana, *The History of the Minor Chāḷukyan Families in Āndhradēśa*, Delhl, 1986 K. Satyanarayana, *A Study of History and Culture of Andhras*, 2 Vols. Delhi, 1975 ; P.V.P. Sastry, *Kākatīyas of Warangal*, Hyderabad, 1978.

2. N. Karashima, Subbarayalu, Y. and Toru Matsui, *A Concordance of the Names in the Cōla Inscriptions*, 3 Vols., Madurai, 1978.

3. Burton Stein, *Peasant Śtate and Society in Medieval South India*, (Oxford University Press, Delhi, 1980) ; Kenneth R. Hall, *Trade and State Craft in the Age of the Chōḷas* (New Delhi, 1980) ; George W. Spencer, *The Politics of Expansion : The Chōḷa Conquest of Śrī Lanka and Śrī Vijaya* (Madras, 1983) ; David Ludden *Peasant History in South India* (Princeton, 1985).

4. D.N. Jha, "Validity of the Brahmana Peasant Alliance,", in N. Karashima (Ed.), *Indus Valley to Mekong Delta : Explorations in Epigraphy* (New Era, Madras, 1985) ; R. Champaka Lakshmi, "Peasant State and Society in South India—Review Article, *Indian Economic and Social History Review*, Vol. 18, Nos. 3 and 4, 1981 ; M.G.S. Narayanan, "Socio-Economic History—New Trends : A Case Study of the Chola Times," Presidential address to the Historiography section, *South Indian History Congress*, Mysore, 1985 ; Kenneth R. Hall, "Peasant State and Society in Chola Times : A View from the Tiniviḍaimarūdur Urban Complex, *Indian Economic and Social History Review*, Vol. XVIII, Nos. 3 and 4, 1981 ; E. James Heitzman, *Gifts of Power : Temples, Politics and Economy in Medieval South sndia*, Unpublished Ph. D. dissertation, University of Pennsylvania, 1985.

5. V. Yasodadevi, *The History of Andhra Country* (Subsidiary) *Dynasties between 1000 A.D. and 1500 A.D.* Published in *Journal of Andhra Historical Research Society*, XVII to XXVII.

6. K.A.N. Sastri, *The Cōḷas* (2nd edn., rev., Madras, 1955).

7. B.V. Krishna Rao, *History of the Eastern Chāḷukyas of Vēṇgī* (Hyderabad, 1974).

8. M. Somasekhara Sarma, "Chāḷukya-Cholulu" (in Telugu), *Telugu Samskriti*, Vol. III, 2nd edn. (Hyderabad, 1982).

9. M. Gift, Siromoney Bhagavandas and S. Govindaraju, "Iconometric Analysis of the Dharmarājaratha" in *Śrīnidhi-Perspectives in Indian Archaeology, Art and Culture* (Madras, 1983) ; Gift Siromoney *et al*, "Temple Carvings of Southern India", in *Perspectives in Computing*, Vol. 5, No. 1, Spring, 1985.

List of Figures and Plates

FIGURES

PLATES

Contents

SECTION II

SECTION—I

1

ON THE SIGNIFICANCE OF A TAMIL RECORD OF KULOTTUṄGA I AT BĀPATLĀ

In the present paper it is aimed to study a Tamil record of the time of Kulōttuṅga I, the first Chāḷukya-Chōḷa ruler of Andhra country, as it would give us an idea about the maintenance of services in the temple, designations and duties of different temple officials. The inscription[1] under study is dated in the 37th year of Kulōttuṅga I's reign, corresponding to A.D. 1107. This record at Bapatla is the Tamil version of a Telugu record[2] of the same place, the texts of which are published in *South Indian Inscriptions*, Volume VI. In this insrciption Kulōttuṅga I is styled as *Samastabhuvanāsraya, Prithvīvallabha, Mahārājādhirāja, Ravikulatilaka, Pāṇḍyakulāntaka, Chōlakulasēkhara, Vīramahēndra, Vikrama Chōla, Paramabhaṭṭāraka, Saptamōviṣṇuvardhana, Rājarājendra, Rājakēsarivarman* and *Tribhuvana Chakravartin.* All these epithets except the last three are not usually met with in his Tamil inscriptions, but are found in most of his Telugu records.[3] Though some of the lines of the record are badly damaged, some of its missing words can be supplemented with the help of the Telugu inscription of the same place. But it is difficult to relate why both the records were left unfinished. It is also not clear as to why these records ended with the words *svastiśrī* abruptly, after the usual imprecatory passage without referring to the name of the scribe of the grant.

The purport of the inscription is to record the donations of king's official named as Mudigoṇḍa Chōḷa Brahmamārāyar. The portion relating to the name of his father and his *gōtra* are damaged. His name suggests that he was a resident of Mudigoṇḍa Chōḷa maṇḍalam, a sub-division of Chōlamaṇḍalam. In the record, it is stated that he gave 10 measures of land to the *dēvakanmis* of the temple of Bhāvanārāyanasvāmy of Bapatla. This gifted land for *Sālābhōgam*[4] was kept in trust of a number of temple officers such as *dēvakanmi, Sthānāpati, Kaṅkāni bhaṇḍāri, Tirumañjana Stōtra,* maid-servants, servants, and dancers of the temple. It was conditioned in the grant that from the land which was given as *Sālābhōgam 30 rājarāja māḍas* should be spent for feeding five learned brahmanas. Further, it is stated that each brahmin should be provided with 4 *Tirumadapalli Kunchamas* of rice daily from the 37th year of the King onwards till the sun and the moon survives. The details of the date of the endowment are mentioned in the record except the Śaka year. It is on Thursday, in the month of *Āṇi* of *Śukla* fortnight and *Saptamīnaksatram.* These details are not to be found in the corresponding Telugu record. At the end of the inscription it is stated that it is a copper plate grant inscribed on stone.

This record is first of its kind in Āndhradēśa to refer to the donation of land for *Sālābhōgamu* being kept in trust of *dēvakanmis* and other temple attendants of the temple. Similarly this record mentions certain temple designations such as *Kaṅkāni, dēvakanmi, Tirumaṇjanam, Tiruvārāyanai* and *Tirumāyi* which are common in usage in the temples of Chōḷa country and new to Āndhradēśa. It is also interesting to note that the gifted land was kept incharge of a number of temple attendants rather than in the trust of either *sthānapāthi* or *dēvakanmi,* the superintendents of the temple. The present record shows that there was only one *Sthānāpati* and *dēvakanmi* in the Visṇu temple at Bapatla. They were Viṣṇuvardhana Paṇḍita and Bhāvanārāyana Brahmamārāyaṇa. The inscription introduces a temple official *Tirumañjanam* Vellaimūrtibhaṭṭu, whose duty appears to decorate the deity of the temple with the religious marks called *Tirumañjanam.* Another temple attendant mentioned in the record is Śrīvaiṣṇava *Kaṅkani.*[5] In the records of the Chōla country *Kaṅkani* is often met with, who acted either as an overseer or as a superintendent of the temple. In addition to these temple officers there is a long list of temple servants (*Parīchārakas*) in the record including dancers and *sānis* of the temple. Their names given in the record were *Parichāraka* Mādhava, *Parichāraka* Śridhara, *Parichāraka* Brahmadēva, *Parichāraka* Nārāyana, *Parichāraka* Mrāna, *Sāni* Nūrava, *Naṭṭavula* Mrāna, *Tirumāyi,* Gaṇḍaparaṇḍi ; *bhaṇḍāri* Rājanārāyana Brahmanārāyaṇa and *bhaṇḍāri* Madhusūdana.

A close study of the names of the temple officers shows that most of them bear only the names of lord Viṣṇu. As the names of *dēvakanmi* and *bhaṇḍāri* given in the record were closely akin to the name of the Tamil officer and donor of the grant, it may be assumed that these two officers came from Tamilnadu and settled in Āndhradēsa.

A record of Śrī Vīrapermādidēva, dated in the 37th regnal year of Kulōṭtuṅga I is noticed at Bhimavaram,[6] which had been registered with the signature of one Pallavarāyar, the minister of the king. Pallavarāyar of this record might be the same as Pallavarāju, who had been credited with several victories over Kaliṅga in a Drākshārāma record[7] of Kulōttuṅga I. In it he was variously known as Vaṇḍuvarāja, Pallavarāja and Tiruvaraṅga and as a resident of Tirunaraiyūrnāḍu, a sub-division of Chōlamaṇḍalam. The Tamil and Telugu records of Mudigoṇḍa Vatsarāyar[8] are noticed at Drākṣārāma dated in the 37th regnal year of Kulōttuṅga I. As the record under study is also dated in the 37th regnal year of Kulōttuṅga I, it is reasonable to suggest that Mudigoṇḍachōla Brahmamārāyar might have come to Āndhrādēśa along with Pallavarāyar and Mudigoṇḍa Vatsarāyar.

Of the place-names mentioned in the grant *Kulōttuṅga Chōlamaṇḍalam* and *Uttamachōla Valanāḍu* were the administrative divisions of the Chāḷukya-Chōḷa dominions. Kambaināṭṭu is identical with Kammanāḍu corresponding to present day Guntur District. Piraṁpaḷḷi is the same a Prēṁpalli of the Telugu records and can be identified with present day Bapatla wherein the temple for god Bhāvanārāyanasvāmy is located. The place name *Paduvirai* mentioned in the inscription is new and is not generally met with in the other records of the temple. In the corresponding Telugu record it is differently mentioned as Udyavāḍa which is difficult to identify.

Thus the above study provides us information about the different temple officers, their duties and the conditions generally laid down by the donors. It is of much significance to observe the contents of this record as it refers to certain new designations of the temple officials which are not to be noticed from the Telugu records of Āndhradēśa. It is also apparent from this that the Viṣṇu temple at Bapatla was greatly influenced by the Southern school of Vaiṣṇavism popularised by Rāmānujachārya as it had the temple officers like *Tirumañjanam, dēvakanmi, Tiruvārāyaṇa* and *Tirumāyi.*

TEXT OF THE INSCRIPTION (Telugu Version)

1. Svasti samasta bhuvanāśraya śrī Prithvī Vallabha-mahā rājādhirāja para-
2. mēsvara-parama-bhaṭṭāraka-ravikula tilaka-Chōḍa kula-sē (kh) ara-pāṇḍya kulāṅtaka-sama-
3. sta-rājāśraya-rāja-rājēndra-vīra-mahēndra vikrama chōḍa-Vijayābha-rana-sri-rājakēsari-
4. vammān-pemmān-naḍigalu-gaṁggā Kāvērī payyaṁ taṁ-saptamō Vishṇuvardhanulaina śrī (mattri)-

5. bhuvana chakravattin Śrī Kulōttuṅga Chōḍa dēvara-pravaddhan māna-divya saṁvatsa 32 srāhi śrı-

6. .... nu Koḍuku-praśasta ...... na mudigoṇḍa chōḍa brahma mā-

7. (rāyaṇḍu) Kulōttuṁgga Chōḍa maṇḍalamuna Uttama Chōḍa Valanānṭi Kammanānṭid = udyavā-

8. (da) lōni-prēṁpalli-śrī bhāvadēvara guḍi sthānāpati Vishṇuvadhan-na paṇḍitulu-dēvakammin-bhāvanārā-

9. (yeṇa) brahma-mārāyaṇḍunu bhaṇḍāri rājanārāyaṇa brahmamārāyaṇḍunu bhaṇḍāri madhusūda-

10. nuṇḍunu tirumañjana (velli) mūttin bhaṭlunustōtra Kēśava bhaṭlunu Śrī Vaishṇava-Kaṁggāni Chīrāmana-

11. bhaṭlu sāni Nūrava-Dārakayu-tribhuvana yeṛi ....bāve yāyaka-Jillava Nūrakayu-Prō-

12. lava-Gōkayu Atyava Gōkavayu Eriyava Kāṭakayu-Kommava Mrānakayu-Mrānava-

13. Kāmakayu-Kāmava Kāṭekayu-Nūrava .... Yākayu-Brammava Mrānakayu-Eṛi-

14. Yava Kraṁtiyu Mrānava Nūrakayu-Nūrakayu-Mrānava.........Kayu Ma(nni)va Jallakayu-Mallava-

15. Eṛiyakayu-(na) yava Pe (nnaka) yu-Nūrava Ponnakayu-Ponnava Mārakayu-Ponnava Mrānakayu-

16. Nūrava N(aṁgga)yu muduvana Kāvakayu Kēśava Mallakyu-Malliva Prōlavayu-Malla-

17. Va Jaggavayu-Vīrava Kāmakayu-Pōnava Eriyayu-Nūrava Jaggavayu-Chaduka-tirumala ka

18. Yu-Naṭṭavula Mrānayayu-Parichāraka Madhavaṇḍu Parichāraka Brahmadēvaṇḍunu-Parichā-

19. raka Nārāyanuṇḍunu-Parichāraka Mrānavaṇḍunu-Parichāraka Śrī-dharuṇḍunu-tirumāyi gāvala-

20. Gaṇḍaparaṇḍiyu Rāghavuṇḍunu-Dāmayayu-berasina-padipādamūla-paṭṭuḍa-Pañchāchāyyan-

21. dēvakammulamu mudigoṇḍachōḍa Brahma mārāya-ri-che-Sālābhō-gamunaku Pemmāṇḍi ko-

22. Rājarāja māḍalu muppadiyuṁ-jēkoni Chandrāditya va (re) nitya aivuru apūvvin brāhmaṇulaku (mṛi) ṣṭānna bhōja (na)-

23. munaku-nokkaniki-tirumaḍapalliki-acheḍi kuṁchamu (౬) padininālugu kumchamulu . . .

24. kuṁchamulu iruvadi (gā) nella kālamu nadapaṁ galavāramu-īpadlalo . . . vara-

25. mu ī māgganmu nadapaṁggalavāramu Nīrāṁkkayu . . . savvan-

26. ma parichā i dhamman-mu-pratipāliṁpa gala vāruga sammadinchi ichchi i-māggan-mu-ta . . .

27. bānarāsi vachchina vāramu gaṁgga karuta kavula pasuramu vadhiiṁchina vāramu pe-

28. Koḍuku kapālamuna guḍichinavāramu sāni vāri vamsśnvayamulu āchaṁdrākkan-mu naḍapaṁ-

29. (ṁgala) vāramu tāṁbra śāsanamu śilā likhitamu . . .

30. dēvagammulamu svasti śaka varushaṁbulu . . . . nti pra.[9]

NOTES AND REFERENCES

1. *S.I.I.*, Vol. VI, No. 201.
2. *Ibid.*, No. 200.
3. *Ibid,*, Vol. IV, Nos. 1263, 1281, 1302, 1334.
4. It is the endowment of land for the maintenance of rest houses and choultries ; See *Tamil Lexicon*, Vol. II, Part I, p. 1390.
5. *Kaṅkāṇi* is a Tamil word and its meaning is given as an overseer, supervisor or a superintendent of the temple in the *Tamil Lexicon*, Vol. II, Part I, p. 684.
6. *S.I.I.*, Vol. V, No. 59.
7. *Ibid,*, Vol. IV, No. 1239 ; *Ep. Ind.* Vol. XXII, No. 23.
8. *Ibid.*, Nos. 1288, 1337, 1339, 1339-A.
9. Left unfinished.

2

INSCRIPTIONS OF ŚRĪ VĪRAPEMMĀDI DĖVA FROM SARPAVARAM AND BHIMAVARAM (A POLITICAL STUDY)

In the last quarter of the 11th Century A.D. i.e., 1076 A.D. Kulōttuṅga I initiated his rule in Āndhradēśa by appointing his sons as the viceroys of Vēṅgı.[1] The sons of Kulōttuṅga I by Madhurāntaki-Rājarāja Chōḍa Gaṅga, Rāja Rāja Mummaḍi Chōḍa and Vīra Chōḍa as well as by Rājēndra Chōḍi-Parāntakadēva appear to have been sent by Kulōttuṅga I to govern Āndhradēśa as the viceroys. Their rule in Āndhradēśa is attested by their records like Ellore, Ṭēki, Chellūru, Pithapuram and Mallavaram copper plates[2] and the stone records at Drākṣārāma, Mukhalingam, Bezawāda and Juttiga.[3] Several theories have been advanced by scholars regarding the period of viceroyalties of the sons of Kulōttuṅga I, particularly after the second viceroyalty of Vırachōḍadēva. A close study of the records of the viceroys in Āndhradēśa during the reigning period of Kulōttuṅga I, i.e., from 1076 to 1118 A.D. reveals a gap of roughly 18 years, i.e., from 1092-93 A.D. to 1111 A.D.[4] This gap falls in between the viceroyalties of Vıra Chōḍa and Parāntakadeva. Corresponding to this period appear the records of one Śrī Virapemmāḍi Dēva[5] and 5 queens, dated in the regnal years of *Sarvalōkāśraya Śrī Viṣṇuvardhana Mahārāja.* Late Sri Mallampalli Somasekhara Sharma considered him a son of Kulōttuṅga I.[6] Late Sri B.V. Krishna Rao who made his studies in this period ignored totally the records of Śrı Vīrapemmāḍi Dēva. He thinks that Velanāṭi Rājēndra Chōḍa I and Kōna Rājēndra Chōḍa I were appointed as the viceroys of Vēṅgi from A.D. 1094 to A.D. 1106 and A.D. 1107 to A.D. 1110 respectively.[7] Dr. N. Ramesan also ignores the records of Śrı Vīrapemmāḍi Dēva and thinks that Vīrachōḍa reigned for 24 years as the viceroy of Vēṅgī i.e., from 1088 to 1111 A.D.[8] Prof. K.A.N. Sastri[9] placed Vikramachōḷa as the viceroy of Vēṅgī from 1093 to 1118 A.D. on the basis of the *Praśasti* of the records of Vikramachōḷa after he became the Chālukya-chōla ruler and a late stone record i.e., the Pithapuram pillar inscription. T.N. Subrahmaniam[10] while editing the two Tamil records from Drākshārāma suggests a gap between the viceroyalties of Vīrachōḍa and Parāntakadēva, i.e., from 1093 to 1111 A.D. The present paper, therefore, aims at making a comprehensive study of the position of Śrī Vīrapemmāḍi Dēva with the aid of the stone records from Sarpavaram and Bhimavaram of the East Godavari district of Andhra Pradesh.

There are 6 stone records from Sarpavaram[11] and 2 stone records from Bhimavaram[12] mentioning the name of Śrī Vīrapemmāḍi Dēva, of which 3 are his personal grants and the rest register the gifts of his five queens. In one grant,[13] he assumed the usual Eastern Chāḷukyan epithets such as *Sarvalōkāśraya* and *Śrī Vishnuvardhana Mahārāja.* In the remaining grants, Śrī Vīrapemmāḍi Dēva was mentioned as a different person from that of *Sarvalōkāśraya Śrī Viṣṇuvardhana mahārāja* in whose regnal years all the records have been dated. The major problem in ascertaining the position of Śrī Vīrapemmāḍi Deva is the complete absence of the Śaka dates in the records and the identification of Viṣṇuvardhana Mahārāja. His earliest record is dated in the 3rd regnal year and the latest in the 37th regnal year.[14] A close study of the dated (in Śaka year) and undated grants of Śrī Viṣṇuvardhana Mahārāja from Drākshārāma, Sarpavaram, Bhīmavaram, Juttiga, Ghantasala and Selapadu indicates the fact that none except Kulōttuṅga I, who could be identified with Viṣṇuvardhana Mahārāja or with Saptamō Viṣṇuvardhana, reigned for a great length of time, i.e., for about 49 years.[15] On this basis the 37th regnal year appearing in the records of Śrī Virapemmāḍi Dēva may safely be assigned to the reigning period of Kulōttuṅga I, by which, it would correspond to 1107 A.D. This supposition may be verified from the evidence of a record from Bhīmavaram.[16] It states that Śrī Virapemmāḍi Dēva entered the town Bhimavaram and after being seated had listened to the several requests of the citizens of the town. He then ordered that the taxes such as *antarāya, veṇḍāya* and *Samastāya* which were being collected from the wet lands (*Tuṇinēla*) from the 31st year to the 33rd year which would amount to 27 *māḍas* may be given to God Viṣṇu. The same gift has been registered with the signature of one Pallavarāyar,[17] who accompanied Śrī Vīrapemmāḍi Dēva to Bhimavaram. Pallavarāyar might be the same as Pallavarāju, who had been credited with the several victories over Kaliṅga in a Drākshārāma record[18] of Kulōttuṅga I dated in the 33rd regnal year of the king. In that record he was variously known as Vaṇḍuvarāja, Pallavarāja and Tiruvaraṅga and a resident of Tirunaraiyurnāḍu, a sub-division of Chōḷamaṇḍalam. It was stated in the record that he subjugated the Kaliṅga country defeating Dēvēndravarman, and planted a pillar of victory on the borders of the ōḍra country. Pallavarāja described in this record might be the same as Karuṇākaran or Toṇḍaimān, the hero of the Tamil *paraṇi* work, i.e. *Kaliṅgattupparaṇi*, as the period and activities of both are identical. On the basis of this evidence, i.e., Pallavarāyar, who is associated with the gift of Śrī Vīrapemmāḍi Dēva, the records of Vīrapemmāḍi Dēva may as well be placed in the reign period of Kulōttuṅga I.

The year 3 mentioned in the Sarpavaram stone record[19] could have been the 3rd regnal year of the viceroyalty of Śrī Vīrapemmāḍi Dēva, as some of the records of the other Viceroys of Vēṅgī[20] have been issued in their own regnal years. With this probability of issuing the records either in the regnal years of Kulōttuṅga I or in the regnal years of one's own viceroyalty, the year 3 mentioned in the Sarpavaram stone inscription, which registers the gift of Mīnava Mahādēvī, wife of Śrī Vīrapemmāḍi Dēva can be assigned to the regnal years of the viceroyalty of Śrī Virapemmāḍi Dēva. By this 3rd year of the record would correspond to 1096 A.D.

From the facts that are collected it is very difficult to assess the position of Śrī Vīrapemmāḍi Dēva. None of the copper plate grants of the time of Kulōttuṅga I and his Tamil record mention the name of Śrī Vīrapemmāḍi Dēva either as a son or as a viceroy of Vēṅgī. The term *Pemmān naḍigal* appears in the *praśasti* or several Telugu stone records of Kulōttuṅga I,[21] along with the usual Eastern Chāḷukyan epithets, *Sarvalōkāśarya*, *Śrī Viṣṇuvardhana Mahārāja*. Thus it would appear at the first sight that Śrī Vīrapemmāḍi Dēva of the inscriptions under review must be identical with Kulōttuṅga I. But on the basis of the names of the queens of Śrī Vīrapemmāḍi Dēva, he can be differentiated from Kulōttuṅta I. The queens mentioned in the Sarpavaram records are Chōḍava Mahādēvī, Mīnava Mahādēvī, Āṇḍāru Cembiyaṁ grānaḍlu, Kavirāja Mahādēvī and Vallavaṁ grānaḍlu who are different from the queens of Kulōttuṅga I. Though it is not possible to identify Śrī Vīrapemmāḍi Dēva of the Sarpavaram and Bhimavaram records, there need be no doubt about his identify as another son of Kulôttuṅga I as well as the viceroy of Vēṅgī. The records of the other viceroys of Vēṅgī described them as *Sarvalōkāśraya* and *Śrī Viṣṇuvardhana Mahārāja.*[22] Thereby it is sufficient to suggest that Śrī Vīrapemmāḍi Dēva was probably a son of Kulōttuṅga I who assumed the usual Eastern Chāḷukyan titles just like the other sons of Kulottuṅga I.

From the review of the Sarpavaram and Bhimavaram records it is evident that :

(1) Sarvalōkāśraya Śrī Viṣṇuvardhana Mahārāja mentioned in the records is no other than *Saptamō Viṣṇuvardhana* or Kulōttuṅga I.

(2) Śrī Vīrapemmāḍi Dēva appearing in the records might have been a viceroy of Vēṅgī from A.D. 1092-93 to 1107.

(3) Śrī Vīrapemmāḍi Dēva might have been a son of Kulōttuṅga I as he reckoned his own regnal years as well as the regnal years of Kulōttuṅga I in his records.

Contrary to the view of Prof. K.A.N. Sastri that Vikramachōḷa succeeded as a viceroy of Vēṅgī after Vīrachōḍa, none of his records are traced from Āndhradēśa during the years A.D. 1092 to 1118 A.D. The Piṭhāpuram pillar inscription of Mallapadēva[23] dated in the year 1202 A.D. and the Erāṟupalli grant[24] of Viṣṇuvardhana dated 1179 A.D. are the only two records which state that subsequent to the departure to protect the Chōḍa country of *Tyāgasamudra*,[25] Vēṅgī became devoid of a king (*Vēṅgībhūmi=nāyaka-rahita jāta*). Some of the Tamil records of Vikramachōḷa[26] credits him with the war against Kaliṅgam and Teliṅga Bhīman. Similarly, Parāntaka Pāṇḍya[27] and Velanāṭi Chōḍa I[28] have also been credited with the similar conquests. On this basis K.A.N. Sastri has suggested that Vikramachōḷa participated in the 1st Kaliṅga invasion which ended by 1098-99 A.D. Unfortunately, there are no records of Kolanu Bhīma in Āndhradēśa to fix up his date. A close study of the records of the Velanāṭi chiefs[29] and the Koṇḍapaḍumaṭis[30] it would be clear that a definite war took place against the region of Kaliṅga during the reigning period of Vikramachōḷa as a king. Hence it can reasonably be surmised that probably these conquests over Kaliṅga and Kolanu could have occurred not during his viceroyalty but during his reigning period. This has been corroborated by the absence of the records of Vikramachōḷa in Āndhradēśa as a viceroy.

It appears that by the end of the reigning period of Kulōttuṅga I there was a war in between the two brothers, Parāntaka and Vikramachōḷa for the Chōḷa throne.[31] Probably in that war, Vikramachōḷa could have emerged as a victor and left the Vēṅgī country to ascend the Chōḷa throne. That might have been stated in the Erāṟupalli record and Pithapuram pillar inscription as his departure from Vēṅgī had resulted into a state of anarchy in Vēṅgī.

The view that Velanāṭi Rājēndra Chōḍa and Kōna Rājēndra Chōḍa were the viceroys of Vēṅgī after Vīra Chōḍa, is not reasonable as Kulōttuṅga I had bestowed the several regions in Āndhradēśa to his generals and ministers as the hereditary possessions for their services to him, among which the Velanāṭi Chōḷas and the Kōna Haihayas attained the Vēṅgī 1600 and the

Kōna *rāshtra.* The rising of position of the generals to the *māṇḍalika* status by bestowing on them the *Pañchamahāśabdas* and insignia of royalty could not be confused with the appointment as the viceroys of Vēṅgi. The view of Late Sri B.V. Krishna Rao in identifying Vikramachōḷa alias *Tyāgasamudra* with Parāntaka Chōḷa is also baseless as Vikramachōḷa was the son of Kulōttuṅga I by Madhurāntaki[32] whereas Parāntaka was his another son by Rājēndra Chōḍi.[33]

It may therefore be said that the view of late Sri Mallampalli Somasekhara Sarma holds good in suggesting the position of Śrī Vīrapemmāḍi Dēva after the second viceroyalty of Vīrachōḍadēva and before that of Parāntakachōḷa.

NOTES AND REFERENCES

1. For a different opinion, that Kulōttuṅga I was the ruler in Vēṅgi from after the death of his father Rājarāja Narēndra, see Dr. N. Venkataramanayya, *The Eastern Chālukyas of Veṅgī*, pp. 296-297.
2. *A.R.E.* 1921-22 ; Part II, para 6, p. 97 ; *Ep. Ind.*, Vol. VI, No. 35 ; *S.I.I.*, Vol. I, No. 39 ; *Ep. Ind.*, Vol. V, No. 10 ; *A.P.A.R.E.*, ep. pl. No. 1 of 1965.
3. *S.I.I.*, Vol. IV, Nos. 1015, 1017 ; *Ibid.*, Vol. V, No. 1005 ; *Ibid.*, Vol. IV, No. 747 ; *Ibid.*, Vol. X, Nos. 15, 59.
4. A record of Vīra Chōḍa at Mukhalingam (*S.I.I.*, Vol. V, No. 1005) is dated in S. 1024 and in the 38th regnal year of the Eastern Gāṅga ruler, Anantavarma Chōḍa Gaṅgadēva, corresponding to 1102 A.D. The presence of Vira Chōḍadēva at Mukhalingam in the year 1102 A.D. might have been to suppress the rebels in the region of Kaliṅga and to support the claims of Anantavarma Chōḍa Gaṅga Dēva, who was closely related to Kulōttuṅga Chōḷa I.
5. Prof. K.A.N. Sastri refers to the term *Perumān naḍigal* as a title of the Chāḷukya-Chōḷa king Kulōttuṅga I (Colas 2nd edition, 1) 55, p. 330). Kanduri Iswara Dutt refers to the term *Permāḍi* as a term used for a reverend person (*Inscriptional Glossary*).
6. *Telugu Samskriti*, Vol. III, p. 199.
7. *The Eastern Chālukyas of Veṅgī*, B.V. Krishna Rao, pp. 449 and 462.
8. N. Ramesan, *Studies in Medieval Deccan History*, p. 104.
9. K.A.N. Sastri, *Cholas*, 2nd edition (revised), p. 320.
10. *Epigraphia Andhrica*, Vol I, pp. 17, 19.
11. *S.I.I.* Vol. V, Nos. 15, 12, 16, 18, 19, 23.
12. *Ibid.*, Nos. 59 and 83.
13. *Ibid.*, 83.
14. *Ibid.*, Nos. 12 and 18.
15. *S.I.I.*, Vol. IV, Nos. 1224, 1385, 1020, 1322.
16. *Ibid.*, Vol. V, No. 59.

17. In medieval Āndhradēśa, it appears to be a customary practice, when a gift was made, either to summon that to a large number of witnesses or to associate them with the signatures of the ministers.
18. *Ep. Ind.*, Vol. XXII, No. 23.
19. *S.I.I.*, Vol. No. 12.
20. Rājarāja Mummaḍi Chōḍa, the 1st viceroy of Vēṅgi, issued his records in his own regnal years. The Ellore copper plate grant was dated in his 2nd reg. year (*A.R.E.*, 1921-22, Part II, para 6, p. 97). Parāntakadēva, who ruled Vēṅgi immediately after Śri Virapemmāḍi Dēva as a viceroy also issued his records in his own regnal years (*S.I.I.*, Vol. IV, No. 737) as well as in the regnal years of his father, Kulōttuṅga I (*S.I.I.*, Vol. IV, Nos. 1017, 1384).
21. *S.I.I.*, Vol. IV, Nos. 1020, 1384.
22. Rājarāja Mummaḍi Chōḍa, the son of Kulōttuṅga I and the 1st viceroy of Vēṅgi (*A.R.E.* 1921-22, Part II, para 6, p. 97) bore the Eastern Chāḷukyan titles such as *Sarvalokāśraya, Viṣṇuvardhana Mahārāja.* Similarly, Rājarāja Chōḍa Gaṅga (*S.I.I.*, Vol. IV, No. 1016) and Parāntaka Dēva (*S.I.I.*, Vol. IV, Nos. 1269, 1275-A), the other viceroys of Vēṅgi before and after the period of Śri Vira Pemmāḍi Dēva bore the same Eastern Chāḷukyan epithets.
23. *Ep. Ind.* Vol. IV, p. 226, ff. v. 24.
24. *Andhra Bharati* Vol. III, No. 12, p. 353.
25. *Tyāgasamudra* is probably the surname of Vikramachōḍa. In some of his Tamil records and in the literary work *Vikramaśolanūla* he was mentioned with this title.
26. *A.R.E.*, 408 of 1909 ; *A.R.E.* 175 of 1911, *A.R.E.* 157 of 1925.
27. *A.R.E.* 433 of 1924.
28. *Ep. Ind.* Vol. XXIX, No. 32.
29. *S.I.I.*, Vol. IV, No. 681.
30. *Ibid.*, No. 662.
31. *Epigraphia Andhrica,* Vol. I, p. 27.
32. *S.I.I.*, Vol. III, No. 73, p. 159.
33. Cp. No. 1, *R.E.A.P.* of 1965, V 45-48.

3

SOME OBSERVATIONS ON THE BEZAWĀDA STONE INSCRIPTION OF PARĀNTAKA CHOḶA

In the present paper an attempt is made to study in detail the Bezawāḍa stone inscription of Parāntaka Chōḷa[1] and to discuss fully the various problems arising from this record. It has been suggested by Dr.V. Yasoda Devi[2] and late Mr. B. V. Krishna Rao[3] that the king mentioned in the inscription was Kulōttuṅga I and it was issued in his regnal years. The Government Epigraphist opined that the record was issued in the 5th regnal year of Parāntaka Chōḷa and in the 46th regnal year of Śrī Pemmanaḍidēva.[4]

Parāntaka Chōḷa, the son of Kulōttuṅga I by Rājēndra Chōḍi,[5] governed Āndhradēśa for a time as its Viceroy under the rule of Kulōttuṅga I, the first Chālukya-Chōḷa ruler. Excepting the record under study, the rest of the lithic records of Parāntaka Chōḷa are found at Drakshārāma and Bhīmavaram.[6]

The record under study is inscribed on a pillar of the ruined Kanakadurga *maṇḍapa* at the foot of the Indrakīla hill at Bezawāda, Krishna District, Andhra Pradesh. The record consists of 33 lines. The characters are of later Telugu-Kannada, paleographically assignable to the 12th Century A.D. The language used in the record is Telugu verse and prose. *Kanda, vṛittam* and *gīta* metres are mentioned in the record. The inscription is important in more than one respect. The record does not register any gift or donation, but incorporates valuable information relating to the conferring of the *raḍḍikam* of Bezawāda to the *Manḍalika* chiefs of Telugu Pallava family. The inscription starts with mentioning the name of Śrī Parāntakadēva with his eastern Chāḷukyan epithets-*Śrī Sarvalōkāśraya Śrī Vishnu Vardhana mahārājulu* and *Tribhuvana Chakravartin.* The 5th victorious regnal year of

Parāntakadēva and the Śaka year 1037 (*Manmatha*) is mentioned. After the *māṇḍalika* chief Bēta, Boddana is stated to have obtained the *raḍḍikam* of Bezawāda from the son of Rājēndra Chōḍadēva. A long *praśasti* of the Telugu Pallavas is mentioned in the record. It starts with *sakala paarma vaṁśōdbhava, bharadvājagōtra, khaṭvāṅgadhvaja, vṛiṣabhalāñchana, kāñchīpuravara, pallava kulatilaka, pādāṁbujasēvita, annuvakāmakula, sāhasājjuna, sangrāmarāma, chālukyānankakāra, paramaṇḍala cūrakāra*. Then *mahāmaṇḍalika* Bhīma, the younger brother of Boddana is compared with Māṁdhāta and Yayāti in his valour.

In the second half of the record reference has been made to Śaka year 1046 corresponding to 1124 A.D. In that year *rājādhirājarājaparamēsvara paramabhaṭṭāraka ravikula tilaka Satyāśraya vaṁsya Chālukyābharaṇa Śrī Tribhuvana Chakravartin Śrīmatpemmanaḍi dēva* being pleased by the valour of *māṇḍālika* Bhīma, conferred on him the *raḍḍikam* of Bezawāda. In the last verse of the record some part of which is damaged, the word-numeral—*rasōdadhi vāyu pathēṁdu* equivalent to Ś 1046 (=1124 A.D.) is recorded.

Some of the titles of Parāntakadēva mentioned in the record under study are new and they do not figure in the other records of the viceroys. The supreme titles such as *Tribhuvana Chakravartin* and *Rājasarvajña* were assumed by him in the present grant. As none of the other viceroys of Vēṅgī assumed such significant titles and dated their records in their own regnal years as Parāntaka, it may be supposed that he is the heir-apparent to the Chāḷukya-Chōḷa throne.[8] The son of Rājēndra Chōḍa, who conferred the *raḍḍikam* of Bezawāda on the Telugu Pallava chief is identified with the Chōḷa king Rājamahēndra (A.D. 1060-1063), the son of Rājēndra II (1052-1064 A.D.), the younger brother of Rājādhirāja I (A.D. 1018-1064) by Dr. V. Yasodadevi.[8] But this identification is not reasonable. Kulōttuṅga I had the princely name Rājēndra Chōḍa; hence his son may be identified with the reigning Viceroy of Vēṅgī, i.e., Parāntaka Chōḷa in whose regnal years the record is dated, as well as in Ś 1037 (=A.D.1115) and in Ś 1046 (=1124 A.D.). Similarly, the title *Rājasarvajña* refers to Parāntaka Chōḷa reigning at Jananāthapura and not to Vikramachōḷa as suggested by Dr. V. Yasoda Devi.[9]

The main interest of the record lies in the dates given therein. The year 46 is mentioned after one thousand years in the second half of the record. But it was supposed by Mr. B.V. Krishna Rao[10] and Dr. V. Yasoda Devi[11] as the regnal years of Kulōttuṅga I. The Government Epigraphist[12] identified the king mentioned in the record with Vikramāditya VI on the basis of the term *Satyāśraya Vaṁsya*. But Pemmanaḍi dēva can be identified with the Chāḷukya-Chōḷa ruler, Vikrama Chōḷa (A.D. 1118-1135) reigning at that time. Though Vikrama Chōḷa begins to rule the Chāḷukya-Chōḷa empire from A.D.

1118, his records do not appear in Āndhradēśa till the year A.D. 1126.[13] On the other hand, the lithic records of the period are found to be dated in the Chāḷukya-Vikrama era.[14] This shows that during the early years of the reign of Vikrama Chōḷa, part of Āndhradēśa was under the sway of the Chāḷukyas of Kalyāṇa. The epithets that the "king belongs to the family of Satyāśraya,' and *ravikulatilaka* applies easliy to Vikramachōḷa, the son of Kulōttuṅga I, who is an eastern Chāḷukyan prince and the great ruler of the Chāḷukya-Chōḷa empire, than Vikramāditya VI who was never referred to in his records as *ravikulatilaka.* The name Pemmanaḍidēva might have been the respectful term used to refer to Vikrama Chōḷa. In Pithapuram pillar inscription of of Mallapadēva,[15] dated Ś 1124 (1202 A.D.) the same king is referred to as *Tyāgasumudra* and not by his personal name, Vikrama Chōḷa. Moreover, if the record is dated in Kulōttuṅga I's 46th victorious regnal year, it could have been mentioned in the beginning of the record, along with name of Parāntakadēva but not at the end of the record.

With the help of the present record and an undated stone record at Yenamadalakuduru[16] of Krishna District, the genealogy of the early Pallava rulers can be fixed. The Bezawāda inscription provides the namers of 3 *māṇḍalika* chiefs. They were Bēta, Boddana and his younger brother Bhīma. The Yenumalakuduru record states that Keta and Tammubangi were the brothers and Tammubangi got two sons by Bādama—Boddana and Bhima. The present record shows that Parāntakadēva gifted the *raḍḍikam* of Bezawāda to *Mahāmaṇḍalika* Boddana after his paternal uncle Bēta (or Kēta) in the year A.D. 1115. Subsequently the same had been given to his younger brother *Mahāmāṇḍalika* Bhima by Pemmanaḍidēva, who may be indentified with Vikrama Chōḷa in the year A.D. 1124.

Thus the present record sheds new light on some of the political events that took place during the last years of the reign-period of Kulōttuṅga I and the early part of the reign of Vikrama Chōḷa. The importance of the present record under study lies in the fact that this is the earliest stone record of Vikrama Chōḷa in Āndhradēśa after the successful restoration of the country from the Chālukyas of Kalyāṇa, as it is dated in the year A.D. 1124. It also gives us more information regarding the prominent role played by Parāntaka Chōḷa in Āndhradēśa as the viceroy of his father Kulōttuṅga I, as the inscription is dated in the regnal years of Parāntaka Chōḷa alone.

TEXT OF THE INSCRIPTION

1. Svasti śrī savvan-lōkāśraya-Śrī Vishṇuvardhanna-mahārājulu-tribhuvana chakravarttin.
2. Śrī Parāṁittaka dēvara-pravaddhan-māṇa-Vijayarājya-saṁvatsaraṁbulu gu-srā-

3. hi śaka-vashaṁbulu gu nēṁṭi-manmatha saṁvatsaraṁbuna rājasarvajñu-
4. ṇḍu-Jananāthapuraṁbuna-rājyābhivaddhanna-(kōṁ) sukhaṁbuna (rā) jyṁbu-sēyu-
5. chunḍi—tana—anvaya kāṁpul-ainavāri-sakala-parama-vaṁsōdbhava-Bhāradvaja-gōtra (kha)
6. ṭvaungga dhvaja-vṛishabha-lāṁchchana-kāṁchchīpuravarē . . pallava kula-ti-
7. laka-pādāmbuja sē (vi) ta annuva kāmakulu . . . . nōḍi-
8. vaḍi-sāhasājjun-na-saṁgrāma-rāma- . . . . Chālukya-
9. naṁkkakāra-paramaṇḍala-chūrakāra pati . . . . jamuṇḍai-
10. na Śrīmanmatā maṇḍalika-Bo (dda) na . . . . kallattin-
11. lōkattin-palli-yalamiṁda Bezawā (ḍa) . . . .
12. //kaṁḍa// (Rā) jēndra Chōḍadēva tanūju . , . narapāla sekha-
13. runi che rājita yaśu Bēta rāja . . . lu pālu
14. (ku) chēta (Rājamahēndru-chēnā-puraṁddara . . . . tā
15. khila kīttin (che) Bezawāda raḍḍikamunu . . . . saluvatti
16. prati pannikulu //va// visēsha padātthaṁbu . . . himāspadu-
17. lai—māṇḍalika Boddaṇḍunuṁ—Tammu . . . .
18. (ka) ṁbu rājyaṁbu sēsi maṇḍalika Boddaṇḍu . . . ṭṭi kaluṇḍu-
19. //vṛi// ātani-tammuṇḍu anvaya viyattala mitruṇḍasesha diktaṭa khyāta yaśōttin Bhī(ma)-
20. ṇḍu sukha sthiti rājai-yabdhi veshṭhi takshma tala nāthu lellan= arigāṁpula-māḍki-
21. na tīru veṭṭa Māṁdāta Yayāti Vēnu nṛiga dhamman-julaṭlati pragal-bhuṇḍu-ai
22. //Gi// para mahīsulu bhaktulai=paṁppaṁ=panulu sēyuchuṇḍaṁ ggaṁda panu
23. rasmiyunuṁ gāḍpu cho (chchin) nachchāna tana yājña so(chchi) veluṁgubhūmi yellanu-
24. Baṁggena Bhīmaṇḍalē-svasti-saṁasta-bhuvanāśraya-rājādhirāja-raja-paramē-

25. svara parama bhaṭṭāraka-ravikula tilaka-Satyāśraya vaṁ (sya) Chālukyābharana-

26. Śri tribhuvana chakravattin Śrīmat-Pemman-naḍi-dēvara-divya-sahasra

27. Vashaṁbulu ४ Σ gu-srāhi-śrī Vēṁgī dēśa chāḷukya . . . . ka-kāra-parama-

28. ṇḍala-chūrakāra-patidēva (gurudvija bhaktu laina) kurumaraja-

29. muṇḍaina—mahā maṇḍalika Bhīma . . . . laku mechchi Bezawāḍa

30. raḍḍikaṁbu—ḍayasēsina- //vṛitta// . . . . raṁbu lu-rasōdadhi

31. vāyu—pathēṁdu—saṁkhya-gā . . . nbeza-

32. vāḍa raḍḍikaṁ=paripura—bhēdirāja paramātmuni chēṁ-baḍasenravīndu-

33. nu dharānyun-aṁburāsulu-sadāgati māggnmu-kalgun-aṁttākunu.

NOTES AND REFERENCES

1. *S.I.I.*, Vol. IV, No. 737.
2. *J.A.H.R.S.*, Vol. XXI, p. 83.
3. B.V. Krishna Rao, *Eastern Chāḷukyas of Vēṅgī*, p. 464.
4. *A.R.E.* of 1959-60, p. 23.
5. Cp. No. 1 of 1965 ; N. Ramesan—*Studies in Medieval Deccan History, Copper Plate Inscriptions of the State Museum*, Vol. III, 1972.
6. *S.I.I.* Vol. IV, No. 1384, 1296, 1248, 1269, 1017 ; *Ep. Ind.*, Vol. VI, p No. 219 ; A.R. No. 473 of 1893.
7. Except Rājarāja Mummaḍi Chōḍa whose 2nd regnal is mentioned in the Ellore Copper plate record (*A.R.E.* 1921-22, p. 97) the other viceroys dated their records in the regnal years of Kulōttuṅga I.
8. *J.A.H.R.S.*, Vol. XXI, p. 82.
9. *Ibid.*, p. 83.
10. B.V. Krishna Rao, *op. cit.*, p. 464.
11. *J.A.H.R.S.*, Vol. XXI, p. 83.
12. *A.R.E.* of 1959-60, p. 23.
13. K.A.N. Sastri—Çōḷas, 2nd edition (revised), p. 343.
14. *S.I.I.*, Vol. IV, Nos, 1228, 1212, 1311, 1310, 1308, 1356, 1357, 1358 ; *Ibid.*, Vol. VI, No. 193, 112 ; *Ibid.*, Vol,, X, Nos. 25 and 26.
15. *Ep. Ind.*, Vol. IV, No. 33.
16. *S.I.I.*, Vol. VI., No. 100.

4

INSCRIPTIONS OF DRĀKSHĀRĀMA IN RELATION TO THE CONCEPT OF LORD-VASSAL RELATIONS

The Western Indologists, who studied the medieval South Indian polity were reluctant to see anything feudal in the relationship between the rulers and the chiefs. Burton Stein observed that "fief as a constituted political sub-region of a private military authority was largely absent from medieval South India."[1] He argued that those binding ties of allegiance which characterise Lord- Vassal relationship of Feudal Europe and Japan are missing from medieval South India. However, he is aware of the rare epigraphical references from Drākshārāma in Andhra which indicate the personal loyalty of a subordinate warrior to a superior. Though it is a hazardous exercise to justify the notion of feudalism in medieval South India, the evidence pointed out by Stein would itself show the existence of the 'fief' system in South India. Hence an attempt is made here to highlight the content of those Telugu stone inscriptions at Drākshārāma and to probe the nature of Lord-Vassal relations that existed in medieval Andhra.

On the north wall of the Bhīmēsvara temple between the 5th and 6th pillars, were inscribed the seven epigraphs[2] in Telugu by two scribes—Rājēndrachōḍa Āchāri and Vīra Rājēndrachōḍa Āchāri. These records which are undated do not refer to any gifts or endowments to the temple and are of interest, as they register certain severe vows taken by a few powerful feudatory chieftains of Āndhradēśa. The main purpose of these seven records is to confirm the loyalties of several *mahā maṇḍalēsvaras* to Śrī Parāntakadēva alias *Sarvalókāśraya Śrī Vishṇuvardhana mahārāja*, Kōnērinmaigoṇḍān by taking solemn vows before Bhīmēsvara Mahādēva. The vows were mentioned in very curious terms to Parāntakadēva as "no one be our overlord except Parantaka, if anybody shall command us or our descendants, his wife shall be ours, and if we or our descendants obey the command of any other, except Parāntakadēva, our wife shall be his". Of these records, six inscriptions were issued by the feudatory chieftains and one by a private individual. They were *mahā maṇḍalīsvara* chōḍaya of Oḍḍavādi,[3] Chōḍaya and Sūraya of Bhīragoṭṭam,[4] Bhīmana of Janturunāḍu[5] and Vīrachōḍa of Sarudunāḍu.[6]

The ruler, Parāntakadēva mentioned in the records was the son of Kulōttuṅga I by Rājēndra Chōḍi, the daughter of Yādavarāja of Virāṭa *vaṁsa*.[7] Parāntaka's inscriptions acknowledging the name of Kulōttuṅga I appear in Āndhradēśa till his father's 49th regnal year, indicating that he acted as the viceroy of Vēṅgī up to A.D. 1118.[8] In several of the stone and copper plate inscriptions it is found, that Parāntaka had assumed the supreme titles—*rājasarvajña*, *chakravartin*, *Tribhuvana chakravartin* and *Parakēsariva-rman*,[9] which indicates that he was chosen as the heir-apparent of Kulōttuṅga I, as well as that his administration had the entire approval of his father.

Although it has not been specifically stated anywhere, scholars like K.A.N. Sastri, B.V. Krishna Rao and others have stated that Vikrama Chōḷa ruled as the last viceroy of Vēṅgī, at the end of the reign-period of Kulōt-tuṅga I.[10] B.V. Krishna Rao has even identified Parāntakadēva with Vikrama Chōḷa on the basis of the statement found in Pithapuram pillar inscription of Mallapa Dēva, dated in Śaka 1124 (1202 A.D.) which states that "after the marvellous Kulōttuṅga had ruled for fifty years, the five *drāviḍas* together with the Andhra country, when *Tyāgasamudra* went to rule the Chōḷa country, the land of Vēṅgī at once fell into a state of anarchy (*Vēṅgī bhūmi-nāyaka-rahita-jāta*).[11] Excepting this record, none of the con-temporary or even late records refer to the above statement, that *Tyāgasa-mudra* alias Vikrama Chōḷa went to the Chōḷa country after fifty years of the rule of his father, Kulōttuṅga I, which caused a state of anarchy in Vēṅgī country.

Vikrama Chōḷa was a son of Kulōttuṅga I by a Hoysāla princess[12] and a claimant to the Chōḷa throne. He came to the throne on 29th June, 1118 A.D. As Parāntakadēva, the heir-apparent continued to rule Vēṅgī even after that date, and was alive on or about 7th May, 1119 A.D.[13] i.e., more than ten months after the date of the accession of Vikrama Chōḷa, it cannot be stated either that Parāntakadēva and Vikrama Chōḷa were identical or that Vikrama Chōḷa was chosen by Kulōttuṅga I to the Chōḷa throne because of the demise of Parāntakadēva. There are three stone records at Drākshā-rāma[14] issued by Siṅgala-p-piḍārar, the minister of the Ceylon king, Vikrama-bāhu. These are dated in the 43rd and 49th regnal years of Kulōttuṅga I, which would correspond to A.D. 1112-13 and A.D. 1118-19 respectively. These records mention the name of the local ruler, i.e., Parāntakadēva and show that the king of Ceylon was on good terms with Kulōttuṅga I.[15] The presence of the Ceylonese minister at Drākshārāma during this period would indicate that, he was there to help Parāntaka either to arrest the advance of the Western Chāḷukyan armies into Andhra or to help the contestant Parāntakadēva to the Chōḷa throne, supported by the ruling monarch, i.e., Kulōttuṅga I against Vikrama Chōḷa.

An inscription at Drākshārāma, dated Ś 1034 and the 43rd year of Kulōttuṅga I registers the lamp donation of Sejjamadēvī, the wife of Sūraparāju of Bhīragoṭṭam.[16] On the basis of this inscription, the undated record of *Mahā maṇḍalēsvara* Sūraparāju registering the oaths of fealty may be approximately dated to the period between A.D. 1112 and A.D. 1118.

Though it is improbable to seek for the same kind of elements to feudalism as existed in Europe and Japan, one can find those feudal tendencies in medieval South India, if the broad features of its polity are considered. Since the beginning of the rule of Kulōttuṅga I in Āndhradēśa, the entire region was entrusted to the various *māṇḍalika* chieftains, who were raised to such a status from generals and military chiefs by conferring on them the *panchamahāśabdas* as well as the hereditary ownership of certain tracts. The five instruments which were associated with *panchamahāśabdas* were *śṛinga* (horn), *tammaṭa* (haliage), taber, *śaṅkha* and cymbal (gong). This was conferred only on very powerful and influential feudatories who had to assume certain obligations to the king. Inscriptional evidence of the period shows that these *māṇḍalika* chiefs had often participated in the various battles to help their overlords and held administrative rights over their areas of rule. The *mahāmaṇḍalēsvaras* often created sub-vassals by granting villages and lands to smaller chiefs, which was generally done with the approval of the supreme lord.[17] Several inscriptions in coastal Andhra mention sub-chiefs along with the names of their immediate chiefs and the supreme lord.[18] Further, in majority of the records of the feudatories, the name of the overlord is mentioned.[19] The omission of the name of the overlord in their records may be due to the weakness of the rulers.

The significance of the records of Drākshārāma under study can be more fully appreciated in relation to certain known political events in the history of medieval Andhra. Anantapāla *daṇḍanāyaka*, the commander-in-chief of the Western Chāḷukyan armies assumed the title of *Chóla kaṭaka chūrakāra*, after defeating a certain *kumāra* in the battle of Jananāthapura.[20] This shows that Parāntaka (*kumāra*-prince) was defeated by the Western Chāḷukyan armies. Vikrama Chōḷa ascended the Chōḷa throne probably with the support of Hōysāla Vishṇuvardhana and his ally, Vikramāditya VI, the Western Chāḷukyan ruler. For this reason, though Vikrama Chōla came to the throne in A.D. 1118, his rule in Vēṅgī was delayed for eight years because of the Western Chāḷukyan domination in Āndhradēśa.[21] It is also evident from the inscriptions that Vikrama Chōḷa was able to re-establish his hold in Vēṅgī, only after the death of Vikramāditya VI in A.D. 1126.[22] From this brief account of the political events of the period, it can be said that the *mahā maṇḍalesvaras* registered their loyalties at the temple of Drākshārāma, to safeguard the interests of their liege-lord, Parāntakadēva against the other claimant to the Chōḷa throne i.e. Vikrama Chōḷa.

It has been considered by Prof. Marc Bloch that the ties of obedience and protection which bind man to man is an important feature of feudal society.[23] Coulborn considers this lord-vassal relationship to be the essential feature of the government in a feudal state, not the relation between the ruler and the subject, not the state and citizen".[24] The oaths of fealty rendered by the *mahā maṇḍalesvaras* in the presence of God Śiva show that the vassals were completely subject to their lord. These oaths might have been taken by them to ensure their lord, in the most effective manner of the fulfilment of their duties as the vassals.

Another instance of showing fealty by the sub-vassals of the Velanāṭi chief, Gonka is known from a Drakshārāma inscription.[25] Though some lines are lost in the inscription, it provides valuable information as regards to the swearing of few persons in the presence of Velanāṭi chief, Gonka as well as before the *raṭṭoḍis* of the village Naḍukuduru, Paṁballivāḍa, Beṇḍavipūṇḍi, Vaikhamūru, Māviṇḍi, Āṇḍapuri, whose names were given. Chōḍa Gaṅga Dēva, the Viceroy of Vēṇgī and the liege-lord as well as the name of the supreme lord, i.e., Kulōttuṅga Chōḷa and his regnal years are mentioned in the inscription.

Thus an analysis of the records at Drākshārāma against the background of the political events that took place show that in its general aspects the concept of feudalism can be successfully used for an understanding of the medieval South Indian polity. The various traits of political feudalism shown above, are comparable to the feudal society of medieval Europe.

NOTES AND REFERENCES

1. Burton Stein (Ed.), "The State and The Agrarian Order in Medieval South India—A Historiographical Critique," *Essays on South India* (*Vikas*, Delhi), 1976, p. 85 ff.
2. *S.I.I.*, Vol. IV, Nos. 1269, 1270, 1271, 1272, 1273, 1274, 1275-A.
3. *S.I.I.*, Vol. IV, No. 1269.
4. *Ibid.*, No. 1270, 1271.

5. *Ibid.*, No. 1272.
6. *Ibid.*, No. 1274.
7. *A.P.A.R.E.*, Cp. No. 1 of 1965 ; N. Ramesan, *Studies in Medieval Deccan*, Hyderabad, Pl. VI, 1.2 (1973).
8. *S.I.I.*, Vol. IV, Nos. 737, 1384, 1296, 1246, 1226.
9. *Ep Ind.*, Vol. XXXII, No. 22 pp. 185-196.
10. K.A.N. Sastri, *Çōlas* (2nd ed. rev.), p. 320. Later he revised his views and concedes to the fact that Parāntakadēva was ruling over Veṅgi since his accession, i.e., A.D. 1111-1112. See K.A.N. Sastri and T.N. Subrahmaniam, "Two Inscriptions of Parāntaka, Year 9", *Ep. Ind.* XXXI No. 22, pp. 185-196 ; B.V. Krishna Rao, *The History of the Eastern Chāḷukyas of V ngi*, (Hyderabad, 1973), p. 467 ; *Ep. Ind.*, Vol. XXIX, p. 233.
11. *Ep. Ind.*, Vol. IV, No. 33, vv. 22-24.
12. *Ep. Ind.*, Vol. XXXII, pp. 227-28.
13. *S.I.I.*, Vol. IV, No. 1226.
14. *Ibid.*, Nos. 1246, 1227, 1225.
15. *Epigraphia Andhrica*, Vol. I, pp. 15-29.
16. *S.I.I.*, Vol. IV, No. 1327.
17. *S.I.I.*, Vol. IV, Nos. 943, 945, 1070 ; Vol. X, Nos. 212, 179, 172, 176, 136, 109.
18. *S.I.I.*, Vol. Nos. 1100, 1114, 1174.
19. *Ibid.* Nos. 1113, 1142 ; Vol. VI, Nos. 123, 153.
20. *Ibid.*, Vol. IX, Part I, No. 212 ; *A.R.E.*, 1906, Part II, para 39.
21. *S.I.I.*, Vol, IV, Nos. 1228, 1229, 1216 ; *Ep. Ind.*, IX, p. 261.
22. *A.R.E.*, 153 of 1897 ; *Ep. Ind.*, Vol. VI, p. 225.
23. *Marc Bloch, Feudal Society* (London, 1961), p. 446.
24. R. Coulborn (Ed.) "The Idea of Feudalism" in *Feudalism in History* (Princeton, 1956), p. 5.
25. *S.I.I.*, Vol. IV, No. 1174.

5

TAMIL INSCRIPTIONS FROM DRĀKSHĀRĀMA A STUDY

In the present paper an attempt is made to study in detail the Tamil records of Drakshārāma, as they throw fresh light on the political events that took place in the last years of the reign-period of Kulōttuṅga I. There are altogether eleven Tamil records at Drākshārāma[1] and are inscribed on the walls of the Bhīmēsvara temple at Drākshārāma in Ramachandrapuram taluk of East Godavari District, Andhra Pradesh. The texts of the records[2] are published in the *South Indian Inscriptions*, Volume IV. Of them five records[3] are fragmentary and do not yield much information. Two Tamil inscriptions of Kulōttuṅga I[4] are published in *Epigraphia Andhrica*, Volume I by T.N. Subramaniam.

It is interesting to note that some of the records[5] under study are ended with the name of the scribe written in Telugu characters. However, the records are dated in the regnal years of Kulōttuṅga I and not in the regular Śaka era, like the Telugu records[6] of the same king. They range from his 25th regnal year to 49th regnal year. Two Tamil records[7] mention the chief queen of Kulōttuṅga I as *Bhuvana muḻududaiyāl* or *Avani muḻududaiyāl*, i.e., "the mistress of the whole world," and not by name. We find such type of references to the chief queen, Madhurāntaki in the Tamil records of Chōḷa-maṇḍalam and not in any of the Telugu records of the king in Āndhradēśa.

In the 40th regnal year of Kulōttuṅga I Valavanmāttāṇḍa Mūvēnda-vēlān[8] gave 45 cows for a perpetual lamp. In the record it is stated that, he is a resident of *Tenkarainaṭṭu* of *Chōlamaṇḍala* and mentioned the name of the viceroy of Vēṅgī, i.e., Parāntakadēva, the son of Kulōttuṅga I. A Telugu record[9] from the same place in Sanskrit language reveals the name of the same person dated in the 34th regnal year of Kulōttuṅga I. Therein it is stated that he belongs to the Śūdra community and to the family of Śırāla. The content of the record is to register the gift of several lands by Mūvēnda Vēlān for the maintenance of 100 Brahmans of *Tiruvīdhi maṭha*, 20 Brahmans of the *satra* (choultry) and to feed 20 Brahmans of the temple. For that purpose, he bought the village Krundūru of *Guddavādināḍu, Pannasakshētra* in Babbaravāḍa, the village Ālavelli free of all taxes, Kollimeli *raṭṭaḍamu*, 20 *puṭṭis* of land in Chintapalli of *Rājarāja Chaturvēdimaṅgalam* and gifted them to the temple. Another Tamil record of him is at Bezawāda,[10] dated in the 41st year of Kulōttuṅga I. It registers the gift of a lamp to Mallēsvaradēva of Bezawāda alias *Rājēndracholāpuram*. A Telugu record of Pallavarāyar[11] at Drākshārāma dated in the 33rd regnal year of Kulōttuṅga I is in Sanskrit language. In it, Pallavarāyar is mentioned as a resident of Tirunaraiyūrnāḍu, a sub-division of *Kulōttuṅga Chōla Valanāḍu* in the *Cholamanḍalam*. This record speaks of the successful conquest of Kaliṅgam region and also planting the pillar of victory on the borders of Oḍra country. K.V. Subramanya Aiyar identified this Pallavarāja with Karuṇākara Toṇḍaimān, the hero of the Tamil *Paraṇi, Kaliṅgattupparaṇi*.[12] Further, in the Smaller Leiden plates of Kulōttuṅga I, dated in his 20th regnal year Rājēndraśiṅga Mūvēndavēlān and Rājavallabha Pallavarāyan were mentioned as *adhikārin* and *sandhivigrahi* of the king respectively.[13] This shows that *Mūvēndavēlan* was an important Tamil Officer of Kulōttuṅga I and he accompanied Pallavarāyar, the great general of Kulōttuṅga I.

The two Tamil records[14] edited by T.N. Ramachandran provide valuable information regarding the relationship of the Choḷas with Ceylon in the last years of Kulōttuṅga I. Uyyavandān Tiruvannāmalaiyan Vijayabāhu Màsāttu Nāyan, the *Pradhāni* of Vikkiramabāhukkal of *Ilām* (Ceylon) gifted 30 *Vaḍḍi* of land in the salt-pan area in the village Uriliḍapalli, in the 49th year of Kulōttuṅga I to maintain 15 ascetics in the *Mahēsvara maṭha* established on the banks of Gōdāvary.[15] A close study of the Telugu records of the same place reveals that one Siṃgala Bhaḍāru[16] bought the *raḍḍikam* of Vēlpūru free of all taxes for 30 *māḍas* and gifted the same to the *maṭha* established by him to free the religious mendicants coming from various countries. It was dated in the 43rd year of Kulōttuṅga I, i.e., 1112 A.D. T.N. Subramaniam[17] suggested that *Siṃgala-p-piḍārar* of the Tamil records means "the noble lord" from Siṃhala or Ceylon. The terms *piḍārar* or *bhaḍāra* are derived from the Sanskrit word *bhaṭṭāra* meaning, "a noble lord". Hence Siṃgala Bhaḍāru of the Telugu record would mean to be the same as that of the Tamil record. By this, it is clear that a *maṭha* was established by a noble lord of Ceylon at Drākshārāma.

Though none of the records of Vikrama Chōḍa have come to light during the life-time of Kulōttuṅga I, scholars like K.A.N. Sastri,[18] B.V. Krishna Rao[19] and others are inclined to place the viceroyalty of Vikrama-chōḷa in Āndhradēśa at the end of the reign-period of Kulōttuṅga I. B.V. Krishna Rao has identified Parāntakadēva with Vikramachōḷa on the basis of the Pithāpuram pillar inscription of Mallapadēva dated in Ś 1124 (1202 A.D.).[20] Excepting this record, with a vague statement that when *Tyāgasamudra* went to ascend the Chōḷa throne, the Vēṅgī country became devoid of any ruler, none of the contemporary or late records contain any evidence to suggest the viceroyalty of Vikrama Chōḷa in Andhra. Parāntaka-dēva was the son of Kulōttuṅga I by Rājēndra Chōḍi, the daughter of Yādavarāja of Virāṭvaṁsa.[21] He was the viceroy of Vēṅgī from A.D. 1111 to the end of Kulōttuṅga's reign and assumed the supreme titles—*Rājasarvajña, Chakravartin* and *Tribhuvana Chakravartin*,[22] which indicates that he was chosen as the heir-apparent by Kulōttuṅga I.

The records of the Tamil officers[23] and the minister of Vikramabāhu[24] king of Ceylon at Drakshārāma dated from the 40th year to the end of the reign of Kulottuṅga I would suggest that they were there to help the viceroy of Vēṅgī Parāntakadēva in arresting the advance of the Western Chāḷukyan armies or to help the contestant Parāntakadēva to the Chōḷa throne against the claims of Vikramachōḷa. This view gains support from the records under study, as some of them mentioned the name of Parāntakadēva.[25] Further seven undated Telugu lithic records at Drākshārāma[26] register certain severe vows taken by few powerful feudatory chieftains of Āndhradēśa to confirm their loyalty to Parāntakadēva.

A Tamil record[27] of one Mudigoṇḍa Vatsarāyar of *Cholamaṇḍala* registers a gift of lamp to lord Bhīmēsvara in the 46th year of Kulōttuṅga I. His other records[28] are at Drākshārāma in Telugu language and alphabet and ranges from Ś 1027 (1105 A.D.) to the 48th year of Kulōttuṅga I. Of them, two records[29] are land grants. In a record dated in the 36th[30] year of Kulôttuṅga I, it was stated that 20 *puṭṭis* of land was bought by Mudigoṇḍa Vatsarāyar from the *raṭṭodis* of Duggūdi for 20 *rājarājamāḍas*. Another inscription[31] registers the gift of *Silāraṭṭaḍikaṁ* in Kaḍalunāḍu of *Guddavādināḍu* bought by Vatsarāyar for 17 *rājarājamāḍas* for providing the *amudu* to the God of the temple. As the early record of Vatsarāya at Drākshārāma is dated in the 35th year of Kulōttuṅga I, it may be suggested that he accompanied the Tamil military officers Pallavarāyar[32] and Mūvēnda-vēlān[33] whose early records are dated in the 33rd and 34th years of Kulōttuṅga I.

As pointed out earlier, of the 11 Tamil records, five of them were ins-cribed by Sūrāchāri alias Virarājēndra Chōḍa Āchāri of *Dākarēmi*, whose name was written in Telugu characters at the end of the records.[34] From this, it is clear that Sūrāchāri was the official scribe and he had the official name as Vīrarājēndra Chōḍa, obtained from the reigning Chāḷukya-Chōḷa king, Kulōttuṅga I, whose princely name was Rājēndra Chōḍa before he sat on the Chōḷa throne. It may be suggested that though the official scribe had inscribed the records of the Tamil officers in Tamil language and alphabet, he preferred the local language, Telugu, in writing his name at the end of the records.

From the study of the land grants of the Tamil officers, it is evident that, the cost of 20 *puṭṭis* of land is 20 *rājarājamāḍas* and to feed 10 *Śivayōgis*, daily, it requires 35 cows.[35] In a record, it is mentioned that to feed 30 Brāhmaṇas daily in the *maṭha* the village Vēlpūru was bought for 30 *māḍas* and gifted to the temple.[36]

Of the place names mentioned in the records, Drākshārāma is referred to as *Iḍaikaraṁbai* or *Dakkāraṁbai*. *Tenkarainā̤ṭṭu* is an administrative division in Chōḷamaṇḍala on the Southern bank of the country. *Gudda-vādināḍu* in which Drākshārāma was situated is the same as the *Guddavādi Viṣaya* of the Telugu inscriptions.

The foregoing survey has shown that the Tamil officers had not only issued their records in Tamil language but also in Telugu and Sanskrit. It is also clear from the study that the Tamil officers had stayed at Drākshārāma after the successful conquest of Kaliṅga region till the end of the region of Kulōttuṅga I. This may be to strengthen the position of the Vēṅgī Viceroy, Parāntakadēva or to support his claims to the Chōḷa throne. Taking into consideration all the Tamil and Telugu records of Āndhradēśa, there is hardly any basis to suggest that Vikramachōḷa was the viceroy of Vēṅgī before he ascended the Chōḷa throne.

NOTES AND REFERENCES

1. Out of 379 records extinct, eleven are in Tamil language and alphabet. And the rest are in Telugu alphabet, though the language varies.
2. *S.I.I.*, Vol. IV, Nos. 1338, 1023, 1024, 1246, 1285, 1339-A, 1225, 1227, 1292, 1027, 1030, 1289.
3. *Ibid.*, Vol. IV, No. 1292, 1027, 1030, 1289, 1024.
4. *Epigraphia Andhrica*, Vol. I, pp. 15-30 ; *S.I.I.*, Vol. IV, 1246, 1225, 1227.
5. *S.I.I.*, Vol. IV, Nos. 1025, 1030, 1225, 1285, 1289.
6. *Ibid.*, Nos. 1224, 1057, 1281, 1306.
7. *Ibid.*, Nos. 1024, 1285, 1322.
8. *Ibid.*, No. 1023.

9. *Ibid.*, No. 1281.
10. *Ibid.*, Vol. IV, No. 779.
11. *Ibid.*, Vol. IV, No. 1239.
12. *Epigraphia Indica*, Vol. XXII, p. 140.
13. *Ibid.*, No. 35, p. 268.
14. *S.I.I.*, Vol. IV, Nos. 1246, 1225, 1227 ; *Epigraphia Andhrica*, Vol. I, pp. 15-30.
15. *Epigraphia Andhrica*, Vol. I, p. 17.
16. *S.I.I.*, Vol. IV, No. 1248.
17. *Epigraphia Andhrica*, Vol. I, p. 16.
18. K.A.N. Sastri, *Colas*, 2nd edition (revised), p. 320.
19. B.V. Krishna Rao, *Eastern Chālukyas Veṅgi*, p. 467 ; *Epigraphia Indica*, Vol. XXIX, p. 233.
20. *Epigraphia Indica*, Vol. IV, No. 33, VV 22, p. 226.
21. N. Ramesan, *Studies in Medieval Deccan*, VI Plate, l. No. 2.
22. *S I.I.*, Vol. IV, Nos. 737, 1384, 1296, 1246, 1226.
23. *Ibid.*, Vol. IV, No. 1226, 1023, 1339A, 1237, 1290, 1291, 1337.
24. *Ibid.*, Nos. 1225.
25. *Ibid.*, Nos. 1023, 1246, 1225, 1227.
26. *Ibid.* Nos. 1269, 1270, 1271, 1272, 1273, 1274, 1275-A.
27. *Ibid.*, No. 1339-A.
28. *Ibid.*, Nos. 1339, 1288, 1337, 1291, 1290.
29. *Ibid.*, Nos. 1288, 1291.
30. *Ibid.*, No. 1288.
31. *Ibid*, No. 1291.
32. *Ibid.*, No. 1239, *Epigraphia Indica*, Vol. XXII, No. 35.
33. *S.I.I*, Vol. IV, No. 1281.
34. *Ibid.*, No. 1026, 1030, 1225, 1285, 1289.
35. *Ibid.*, No. 1288.
36. *Ibid.*, 1248.

6

RECORDS OF RĀJĀDHIRĀJA AT DRĀKSHĀRĀMA

Kulōttuṅga I, son of Rājarāja Narēndra and Ammāṅga became the master of the eastern Chāḷukyan and Chōḷa dominions by 1070 A.D. As he descended from the Chāḷukya line on the paternal side and the Chōḷa line on the maternal side, the historians designated him and his successors as the Chāḷukya-Chōḷas.

During the rule of the Chāḷukya Chōḷas, a number of local chiefs and *māṇḍalikas* aided the Chāḷukya-Chōḷa rulers in times of need and thus enjoyed autonomous authority in Āndhradēśa. After the rule of Rājarāja II (1146-1173 A.D.), 4 kings reigned in succession on the Chāḷukya-Chōḷa throne, terminating by about 1979 A.D. We have the reigns of Rājādhirāja II (1163-79 A.D.), Kulōttuṅga III (1178-1216 A.D.), Rājarāja III 1216-60 A.D. and Rājēndra III (1246-79 A.D). It is curious to note that the Chāḷukya-Chōla kings mentioned in the inscriptions of the Āndhra area are not always the same as the kings of the Tamil area. The identity of the names of the kings and that of the reign-periods are the same, only in the case of the inscriptions hailing from the present districts of Cuddapah and Nellore. The Drākshārāma records numbering twenty-two and one inscription from Siṁhāchalam which are dated between A.D. 1193 and 1303[1] mention the names of the two kings, viz., Rājādhirāja and Rājarāja. Their identity with the Chāḷukya-Chōḷa kings is disputed on the basis of the dates supplied by the inscriptions. The present paper relates to the records of Rājādhirāja at Drākshārāma and their significance in the reconstruction of the last phase of the Chāḷukya rule in Andhra.

Not much attention has been paid by scholars to these inscriptions owing to the supposition that they do not show the kings' effective authority in the region. The desire of the Kākatīyas to occupy the Coastal Andhra tract evidenced itself early in their career. Prōla II was dead in one of those battles fought for the possession of that area[2]; his son, Rudradēva's inscriptions dated A.D. 1158, 1168 and 1186 are available at Drākshārāma,[3] though dated in the reigns of Rājarāja II and Vishṅuvardhana. It was Rudradēva's nephew Gaṇapatidēva who subdued the Coastal Andhra region sometime before A.D. 1210, which was retained by his successors with occasional losses of the Gōdāvarī valley and the region near Nellore. This has led to the view that it might have been customary for the engravers of inscriptions at Drākshārāma to mention the name of the Chāḷukya-Chōḷa ruler, even though there was no such ruler.[4] It has been suggested by V. Yasoda Devi that the king mentioned in these inscriptions should be identified with the Chāḷukya-Chōḷa king of the Tamil area, in spite of the difference in name.[5]

As against these views, it may be pointed out that, if it were a custom at Drākshārāma, to date the records in the reigns of the Chāḷukya-Chōḷa rulers, it should have been found throughout the series of inscriptions at that place. But we have a number of inscriptions issued by the Durjayas of Velanāḍu,[6] the Haihayas of Kōna-seema,[7] the Chiefs of Kolanu[8] etc., without any reference to the Chāḷukya-Chōḷa ruler. Again, it is inexplicable how the name of the king of Drākshārāma could be different from the king known from the Tamil records on the same date. It is arbitrary to identify Rājādhirāja with Kulōttuṅga III and the like, without much evidence. Moreover, among the Chāḷukya-Chōla rulers, there was none except Kulōttuṅga III, who was credited with the conquest of the Andhra area and occupation of Uraṅgai (Warangal). Even this seems to have been only a raid.

To identify the kings revealed by the inscriptions at Drākshārāma and the solitary record at Siṁhāchalam with the Chāḷukya-Chōḷa kings of the Tamil area, one should find evidence to show that such a practice of mentioning their names was in existence throughout Andhra. But such evidence is conspicuous by its absence at places other than Drākshārāma and Siṁhāchalam. As stated already, the inscriptions located in the Nellore and Cuddapah districts agree with those coming from the Tamil area in respect of kings' names and their periods of rule.

If there is any connection of the kings known from the Drākshārāma inscriptions and the Siṁhāchālam inscription with any of the Chāḷukya-Choḷa rulers, it could be Rājādhirāja II who is known from his Tamil records up to his 16th regnal year. He could have migrated to the area near Drākshārāma after his expulsion from the Chōḷa throne by Kulōttuṅga III, as pointed out by Prof. K.A. Nilakanta Sastri.[9]

Now it is proposed to take the inscriptions between A.D. 1193 and 1303 in the reigns of Rājādhirāja and Rājarāja at Drākshārāma and Simhāchalam to have been issued in the names of kings of a local dynasty was a collateral branch of the Chāḷukya-Chōḷas.

Identifying Rājādhirāja of the Drākshārāma and Simhāchalam inscriptions with *Rājādhirāja II* the rule of this king can be placed between his 28th regnal year (Ś. 1115=A.D. 1193)[10] and 49th year (Ś. 1137=A.D. 1215).[11] This means that the king came to the Drākshārama area between his 16th and 28th regnal years.

Rājādhirāja II was probably succeeded by Rājādhirāja III whose relationship with the former is not known. His inscriptions start from his 36th year (Ś. 1174=A.D. 1252)[12] so that he could be taken to have been the immediate successor of Rājādhirāja II in 1216 A.D. His latest regnal year is the 37th, equivalent to Ś. 1175=A.D. 1253.[13]

Rājādhiraja III's successor was one Rājarāja whose inscriptions refer to Ś. 1176=A.D. 1254[14] 38th regnal year and Ś. 1189=A.D. 1267.[15] He can thus be placed as the ruler between A.D. 1254 and 1267. Here, as well as for the next reign, it is not possible to take the regnal years as those of the concerned kings themselves, because we would be placing the accession of Rājādhirāja III, Rājārāja and the next Rājādhirāja IV at A.D. 1216 itself. Therefore, it may be argued that, excepting the regnal years of Rājādhirāja II which are a continuation of his rule from after his rule in Tamil area, the years of other rulers are the total years of the family's rule and not their regnal years. Therefore the Śaka years are indicators of their duration of rule.

Next to Rājarāja ruled Rājādhirāja IV whose inscriptions may be taken to commence from Ś. 1180=A.D. 1258 (43rd year)[16] and end by Ś. 1225=A.D. 1303.[17] He must have acted as heir apparent during A.D. 1258-67.

The genealogy and chronology of his branch of the Chāḷukya-Chōḷa family may be formulated as follows :

Rājādhirāja	II	(A.D. 1193-1215)
Rājādhirāja	III	(A.D. 1216-1253)
Rājarāja		(A.D. 1254-1267)
Rājādhirāja	IV	(A.D. 1258-1303)

One interesting feature in some of these inscriptions which may justify our surmise of the rule of a branch of the Chāḷukya-Chōḷa dynasty is that close relatives and officers of Kākati Ganapatidēva and Rudramadēvī mention the names of these petty rulers. Rāja Nāyaka, a minister of Rēcherla Rudri Reḍḍi, who was a vassal of Gaṇapatidēva, mentions the 46th year, besides Śaka

1134 (=A.D. 1212).[18] This 46th year was not referred to any king in the record itself. It does not belong to the reign of Kākati Gaṇapati, because he ascended the throne in A.D. 1198. It certainly fits into the reign of Rājādhiraja II who was king of the Tamil areas by about 1163-66. In Ś. 1175=A.D. 1253 which was the 37th year of Rājādhirāja III,[19] Jāyapa Nāyaka the brother-in-law and the general of Kākati Gaṇapati, donates a gift at Drākshārāma. In a similar manner, an officer, of Rudramadēvī mentions Rājādhirāja IV in in Ś. 1200=A.D. 1278.[20] A little later in Ś. 1215=A.D. 1293[21] Induluri Annayya who was matrimonially connected with the Kākatīyas and an officer of the time of Prātāparudra, dates his incription in the reign of Rājādhirāja IV. These instances point, not to the suzerainty of kings named Rājādhirāja over the donors but to the ruler of local kings near Drākshārāma. That the officers of the Kākatīyas chose to mention the local kings shows the semi-independent nature of the rule of the Chiefs in the Gōdāvarī valley like this branch of the Chāḷukya-Chōḷas, the Haihayas of Kōna, the Chāḷukyas of Piṭhāpur, Nidaḍavole, etc.

The above discussion reveals that a collateral branch of the Chāḷukya-Chōla family ruled in the vicinity of Drākshārāma for nearly a century after the authority, effective or feeble, of the Chāḷukya-Chōḷas ended. This rule was mentioned optionally by chiefs or their officers. It has also been shown above that the mention of the name of the king does not necessarily indicate the suzerainty over the donor-chiefs or officers, but points to the rule of the concerned king in the area in question.

NOTES AND REFERENCES

1. *S.I.I.*, IV, Nos. 1223, (*Ś.* 1115) ; 1100 ; 1279 (*Ś.* 1123), 1257 (*Ś.* 1127) ; 1117 (*Ś.* 1134), 1118 (Ś. 1134) ; 1330, (*Ś.* 1137) ; 1043 (*Ś.* 1174) ; 1178 (*Ś.* 1174) ; 1045 (Ś. 1175) ; 1033 (*Ś.* 1175) ; 1230 (*Ś.* 1176) ; 1318 (*Ś.* 1189) ; 1032-A (*Ś.* 1180) ; 1163 (*Ś.* 1188) ; 1373 (*Ś.* 1197) ; 1074, (*Ś.* 11 (99 ?) 1152 (*S.* 1200) ; 1038 (*Ś.* 1210) ; 1079 (*Ś.* 1211) ; 1307 ; (*Ś.* 1215) ; 1183 (*Ś.* 1225) ; *Ibid.* VI, No. 1177.
2. *Ibid.*, IV, No. 1242.
3. *Ibid.*, Nos. 1095, 1107 and 1155.
4. M. Somasekhara Sarma and M.V.N. Aditya Sarma, "The Later Chāḷukyas of Vēṅgi," *J.A.H.R.S.*, XXXII, p. 77.
5. *Ibid.*, p. 79 ; V. Yasodadevi, "The History of Andhra Country—1000 A.D.—1500 A.D. —Subsidiary Dynasties," *J.A.H.R.S.*, XVIII, p. 107.
6. *S.I.I.*, IV, Nos, 1041, 1054, 1066, 1068, 1069, 1365 and 1366.
7. *Ibid.*, Nos. 1046, 1145, 1286, 1315.
8. *Ibid.*, Nos. 1058, 1206.
9. *The Chōlas*, 2nd edition (Madras, 1955), p. 375.
10. *S.I.I.*, IV, No, 1223.

11. *Ibid.*, No. 1330.
12. *Ibid.*, No. 1043.
13. *Ibid.*, Nos. 1033 and 1045.
14. *Ibid.*, No. 1230.
15. *Ibid.*, No. 1318.
16. *Ibid.*, No. 1032-A.
17. *Ibid.*, No. 1183.
18. *Ibid.*, No. 1117.
19. *Ibid.*, No. 1045.
20. *Ibid.*, No. 1152.
21. *Ibid.*, No. 1307.

7

INSCRIPTIONS OF TRIBHUVANA CHAKRAVARTIN RĀJĀDHIRĀJA II

The records with the name of Tribhuvana Chakravartin Rājādhirāja are noticed at Drākshārāma[1] and Siṁhachālam,[2] which are published with the texts in *South Indian Inscriptions* volumes IV and VI. These records are dated in the regnal years of the Chāḷukya-Chōḷa King, Rājādhirāja and in the Śaka years. As stated earlier, even though the names of the rulers differ, scholars, like V. Yasoda Devi,[3] M. Somasekhara Sarma and M.V.N. Aditya Sarma[4] identified Tribhuvana Chakravartin Rājādhirāja of these records with the Chāḷukya-Chōḷa kings of the Tamil area, i.e., Kulōttuṅga III (A.D. 1178-1216), Rājarāja III (A.D. 1216-1260), and Rājēndra III (A.D. 1246-1279). P.V.P. Sastri[5] suggested that the records of the Kākatīya generals like Jāyapa Nāyaka and Indulūri Gunnaya Mantri at Drākshārāma, which mentioned the name of Tribhuvana Chakravartin Rājādhirāja, dated in his regnal years is in the process of respecting the local traditions in the conquered areas. In the preceding pages it has been observed that a collateral branch of the Chāḷukya-Chōḷa family was established in the vicinity of Drākshārāma, whose sway extended as far as Siṁhāchalam in the North for a century, i.e., from A.D. 1193 to 1303. It has also been pointed out that, though the Kākatīyas were powerful rulers in Āndhradēśa, their records were absent to the North of Drākshārāma. In the present paper, an attempt is made to discuss the date of retirement of Rājādhirāja II to the Andhra country with the help of his Punganur record and some of his inscriptions at Drākshārāma.

Rājādhirāja II's accession to the Chāḷukya-Chōḷa throne was not smooth. He was the grandson of Vikramachōḷa and his accession date was calculated earlier by Kielhorn[6] as between the 28th February and 30th March, 1163 A.D. It was followed by many scholars like Robert Sewell,[7] Jacobi[8] and they suggested correcting the regnal years and data in more than 15 records. But later discoveries of inscriptions enabled the scholars to revise it. On the basis of the astronomical data provided in some of the records of the king, Sri N. Sethuraman[9] calculated it as in between June and July of 1166 A.D., which is more convincing. Rājādhirāja II acted as a co-regent with Rājarāja II for sometime i.e., upto 1173 A.D. It is significant to note that after the accession of Rājādhirāja II in 1166 A.D., no records of Rājarāja II are issued in the Tamil districts.[10] But interestingly, the records of Rājarāja II are noticed from several places in Āndhradēśa till the year 1173 A.D.[11]

Probably due to the accession of Kulōttuṅga III in the year 1178 A.D. on the Chōḷa throne or due to the troubles from the side of Pāṇḍyas, Rājādhirāja retired to Āndhradēśa, shortly after his 26th regnal year, i.e., the date of his Punganur inscription.[12] But Prof. K.A.N. Sastri opined that a record of Rājādhirāja at Drākshārāma,[13] which is dated in the 61st regnal year is a mistake for the year 16.[14] On this basis, he placed the commencement of Rājādhirāja's reign in Āndhradēśa from his 16th regnal year, i.e., from 1182 A.D. Sri N. Sethuraman[15] accepted Sastri's surmise and stated that Rājādhirāja ruled in Tamilnadu up to his 15th year and then retired to Andhra in his 15th regnal year.

Kulōttuṅga I was the first Chāḷukya-Chōḷa ruler to assume the title *Tribhuvana Chakravartin.* This title of him is noticed from his records as early as the 5th regnal year[16] in addition to the usual Eastern Chāḷukyan epithets as *Sarvalōkāśraya Śrī Vishṇuvardhana Mahārāja.* It is important to note that the successors of Kulōttuṅga I preferred the title of *Tribhuvana Chakravartin* and are referred to by their personal names in the inscriptions by completely omitting the usual eastern Chāḷukyan titles.

The records of *Tribhuvana Chakravartin* Rājādhirāja at Drākshārāma with the high regnal years ranging up to the 76th year[17] are not considered by the learned scholars. Like the records of Rājādhirāja II, these inscriptions also mention him as *Tribhuvana Chakravartin* P.V.P. Sastri[18] who touched the problem surmised that the Kākatīya minister who issued a record in the name of Rājādhirājadēva, dated in his 76th regnal year should be identified with Rājarāja III and not with Rājādhirājadēva. He further states that by that time the Chāḷukya-Chōḷa king was dead, but only to honour the custom of the place the Kākatīya minister issued the record in the name of the deceased king. But this suggestion is highly unconvincing in the light of a number of records at the same place which were issued without referring to the name or the regnal years of the Chāḷukya-Chōḷa king. Moreover, a record in the name of Rājādhirāja is noticed at Simhāchalam.

All this evidence shows that the historicity of Tribhuvana Chakravartin Rājādhirāja cannot be questioned and it is not the customary practice of the scribes of Drākshārāma temple to mention the names of the Chāḷukya-Chōḷa rulers in only some of the records. Similarly we have not come across any instance issuing the records in the name of a deceased king some 33 years after the end of his reign-period in the history of the Chōḷas, as suggested by Shri P.V.P. Sastri.

The Punganur inscription[19] of Rājādhirāja is peculiarly dated as "the 12th year which was also the 14th year" (*Padinālavadana Pannīrandavaḍu*). The Government Epigraphist explained it as the two regnal years counted from the date of his actual accession and the other from the year of his nomination to the Chōḷa throne by Rājarāja II. But in view of the calculation of the date of accession of Rājādhirāja II as in 1166 A.D. which is generally agreeable, it is difficult to depend on the suggestion made by the Government Epigraphist. The only other alternative is to add up the two regnal years that appeared in the record, as it is generally made in the case of several other Tamil inscriptions. Therefore, the date of the Punganur inscription may be calculated as (14+12) the 26th regnal year of Rājādhirāja II. By this, it is evident that Rājādhirāja was in the Chōḷa dominions during his 26th regnal year i.e., 1192 A.D. But N. Sethuraman[20] opined that Rājādhirāja II issued this record in the 12th year counted from the end of his reign period in the Chōḷa country. Thus he came to the conclusion that Rājādhirāja held his sway in the Chōḷa country for 14 years and after that he retired to the Andhra country on the basis of a Drākshārāma record, the regnal years of which were corrected by him accordingly. Contrary to this, the earliest record of Rājādhirāja II at Drākshārāma is dated in his 28th regnal year.

The Drākshārāma inscription[21] which is considered the main basis in stating that Rājādhirāja II commenced his rule in Āndhradēśa is partly damaged. It refers to the regnal year 61 of Tribhuvana Chakravartin Rājādhirājadēva and of the Śaka year mentioned in the record, the first two numerals are clear as 11 and the rest of it is damaged. But in line No. 2 the chronogram *ratna* is clear. The other details of the date are *Śrāvaṇa Suddha*, 10. On this basis it may be reconstructed as S' 11(99). In support of this another record[22] of the same place and of the same king may be considered. It is dated in Śaka 1200 and refers to the 62nd regnal year of the king. The other details mentioned in the inscription are *Śrāvaṇa Suddha* 15, *Baumavāra*, *Mīnasukrōttare* and the 1st day.

Thus, the study of the records of Tribhuvana Chakravartin Rājādhirāja at Drākshārāma reveals the existence of another king of the same name, whose accession would fall in the year 1216-17 A.D. and shows that the record of Rājādhirāja with 61st regnal year need not be considered as a mistake for the 16th year of Rājādhirāja II.

In this regard it is interesting to note the contents of a record of Kulōttunga III at Thiruvennainallūr,[23] dated 1195 A.D. In it, Kulōttunga requested the reader to prefix the *praśasti* of Rājādhirāja before proceeding to read the text of the grant. It thus clearly indicates that at the time of issuing this gift by the king, Rājādhirāja II was not in the Chōḷa country. In this connection, it may be noted that the earliest record[24] of Rājādhirāja II at Drākshārāma is dated in his 28th regnal year. Therefore, it may be suggested that Rājādhirāja II came and settled in Andhra country sometime between his 26th and 28th regnal year, i.e., 1192-93/94 A.D. and not after his 15th regnal year as assumed by the others.

NOTES AND REFERENCES

1. *S.I.I.*, IV, Nos. 1223 ; 1100 ; 1279 ; 1257 ; 1117 ; 1118 ; 1043 ; 1178 ; 1045 ; 1033 ; 1230 ; 1318 ; 1032-A ; 1163 ; 1373 ; 1074 ; 1152 ; 1038 ; 1079 ; 1307 ; 1183.
2. *Ibid.*, Vol. VI, No. 1177.
3. V. Yasodadevi, "The History of Andhra Country—1000 A.D.—1500 A.D.— Subsidiary Dynasties," *J.A.H.R.S.*, V. XVIII, p. 107.
4. M. Somasekhara Sarma and M.V.N. Aditya Sarma, "The Later Chāḷukyas of Vēṅgi" *J.A.H.R.S.* Vol. XXXII.
5. P.V.P. Sastry, *The Kākatīyas of Warangal*, p. 176.
6. *Ep. Ind.*, Vol. IX, pp. 211-213.
7. *Ibid.*, Vol X, p. 127 ; *A.R.E.* 571 of 1907.
8. *Ibid.*, Vol. XI, p. 123 ; *A.R.E.*, 172 of 1908,
9. Earlier, Sri N. Sethuraman in his book, *The Chōlas Mathematics Reconstructs the Chronology*, (1977), pp. 181-83, surmised that Rājādhirāja II came to the throne between 5th and 8th January 1166 A.D. Later he revised his views and expressed them in *Medieval Pāṇḍyas* (1980), p. 34 ff.
10. K.A.N. Sastry– *The Cōlas* (2nd edition, revised), p. 359.
11. *S.I.I.*, Vol. X, Nos. 187, 184 ; *Ibid.*, Vol. VI, No. 626, 180.
12. *A.R.E.*, 209 of 1932, Part II, para 18.
13. *S.I.I.* Vol. IV, No. 1074.
14. K.A.N. Sastri, *op. cit.*, p. 358.
15. N. Sethuraman, *Medieval Pāṇḍyas*, p. 34.
16. *A.R.E.*, 197 of 1910.
17. *S.I.I.*, Vol. IV, Nos. 1163, 1373, 1074, 1152, 1038, 1079, 1307, 1183.
18. P.V.P. Sastri, *op. cit.*, pp. 176 and 177.
19. *A.R.E.*, 209 of 1932 ; Part II, p. 18.
20. N. Sethuraman, *The Chōḷas—Mathematics Reconstructs the Chronology*, p. 151.
21. *S.I.I.* Vol. IV, No. 1074.
22. *Ibid.*, No. 1152.
23. *Ibid.*, Vol. VII, No. 942 ; Also see N. Sethuraman *op. cit.*, p. 152.
24. *S.I.I.*, Vol. IV, No. 1223,

8

IDENTIFICATION OF VISHNUVARDHANA MAHĀRĀJAS (12TH CENTURY A.D.) OF THE TEMPLE INSCRIPTIONS OF ĀNDHRADĒŚA

In this paper an attempt is made to study the inscriptions of Bhimavaram, Sarpavaram, Drākshāramam, Palivela, Juttiga and Pattisam temples and to identify the kings, who assumed the Eastern Chāḷukyan epithet, *Sarvalōkāśraya Śrīviṣṇuvardhana Mahārāja* with the kings of minor Chāḷukyan families in Coastal Andhra districts who flourished in 12th Century A.D. Kulōttuṅga I, the first Chāḷukya-Chōḷa ruler is referred to in his and his peoples records as *Saptamō Viṣṇuvardhana.*[1] As it has been pointed out by N. Venkataramanaiah,[2] he is the seventh Viṣṇuvardhana Mahārāja counting from the reign-period of Dānārṇava. In this regard it is curious to note that none of his successors were styled as Viṣṇuvardhana *Mahārājas* in their stone records, instead they assumed the title Tribhuvana Chakravartins and were also referred to by their personal names.[3] This might be due to the rising of the several minor Chāḷukyan families in Coastal Andhra districts who wanted to elevate their family status by assuming the usual Eastern Chāḷukyan names and titles, i.e., Vijayāditya and Viṣṇuvardhana Mahārāja.

The stone and the copper plate records of Kulōttuṅga I and his sons[4] reveal that their coronation took place at Jananāthapuri[5] on the banks of the sacred river Gōdāvarī. Interestingly some of the kings of the Chāḷukyan family of Bēta Vijayāditya line also celebrated their coronation at the same place, i.e., Jananāthapuri.[6] And only at a later time, i.e., 1202 A.D. Mallapadēva celebrated his coronation at Piṭhāpuram.[7] Hence the historians generally designated this family as the Chāḷukyas of Piṭhāpuram. From the records of the period it appears that these kings had under their sway Bhīmavaram, Juttiga and Drākshārāma regions.

Kulōttuṅga I, reigned for a long period of about 49 years, i.e., from 1070 A.D. to 1118/1119 A.D. After Kulōttuṅga I, Vikramachōḍa come to the throne, but his records are not noticed in Coastal Andhra Districts till the year 1126 A.D. because of the Western Chāḷukyan expansion in Andhra in this period. Also his records are not very numerous as that of his father and he was referred to in them as Tribhuvana Chakravartin Vikramachōḍa.[8] At Drākshārāma there are 11 inscriptions,[9] mentioning the name of one Viṣṇuvardhana Mahārāja and his regnal years. On calculation his accession took place in the year 1125/26 A.D. Of them six records[10] register the lamp grants of the Queens of the Eastern Gāṅga King Anantavarma Chōḍaganga in the year 1128 A.D. The rest belong to Nūṁkana,[11] minister of Malayamaṇḍala, Sūraparāju[12] of Malayamaṇḍala and the *māṇḍalika* Chief Bhīma Nāyaka,[13] the brother of Boddi Nāyaka. As the date of accession of this Viṣṇuvardhana *Mahārāja* differs with that of the reigning Chāḷukya-Chōḷa king, he cannot be identified with Vikramachōda.

The Eḍarupalli copper plate grant[14] and the Pithapuram pillar inscription of Mallapadēva[15] inform us that Mallapadēva II had married Caṇḍaladēvī, the daughter of Brahma, lord of Sāgara *Visaya*. Their son was Vijayāditya III ; who came to the throne in the Śaka year 1049, corresponding to A.D. 1126-27. But in the records the Śaka year is mentioned in numerical words. It is expressed as *Śākābde nidhi jaladhi Viyatchandra* which may represent the year either S' 1049 or S' 1079. Prof. Kielhorn and E. Hultzsch inclined to think that the date is S' 1079=A.D 1158 as it would bring closer the reign period of Vijayāditya III with that of his son Mallapadēva (III) who came to the throne in S' 1124=1202 A.D. But in the light of the Eḍarupalli copper plate grant, dated in S' 1101 (=1179 A.D.) issued by Viṣṇuvardhana, son of Vijayāditya III, the first Śaka date (S' 1049) appears to be more probable. This Vijayāditya III can be identified with Viṣṇuvardhana Mahārāja of the Drākshārāma records.

At this time Vikramachōḷa undertook a campaign against the Western Chāḷukyas assisted by several *māṇḍalika* chieftains. A record of the Parichchēdi Chief Naṁbaya at Chēbrōle,[16] in the year 1127 A.D. and the 9th regnal year of Vikrama Chōḍa shows that the authority of the Chāḷukya-Chōḷas was restored by 1127 A.D. in the Coastal tracts. Probably either to help the Chāḷukya-Chōḷas in this regard or to visit the pilgrim centre, Drākshārāma, the Eastern Gāṅga king Anantavarma Chōḍagaṅga, who was closely related to Kulōttuṅga I came to Drākshārāma with his harem and offered the lamp grants to lord Bhīmēsvara. It may be suggested in this regard that probably Drākshārāma was under the sway of the minor Chāḷukyan family. Hence the queens of Chōḍagaṅga mentioned Viṣṇuvardhana Mahārāja and his regnal years in their grants instead of the reigning Chāḷukya-Chōḷa king,

Vikrama Chōḍa. His other records are found at Juttiga[17] and Pattisam,[18] wherein his 15th and 21st regnal years are mentioned.

The records[19] of one Viṣṇuvardhana Mahārāja alias Mallapadēva Chakravartin are noticed at Bhīmavaram, whose accession took place in the year 1173-74 A.D. His latest record is dated in his 10th regnal year.[20] He may be identified with the issuer of the Eḍarupalli copper plate record i.e., the son of Vijayāditya III by Lakshmīdēvī dated in 1179 A.D.

An inscription[21] registers the grant of 7 *Khanḍikas* of land for the burning of two perpetual lamps in the temple of lord Rājanārāyaṇa by Vīranarendra, son of Vijayāditya (III) by Lakshmīdēvī. This record is dated in the Śaka year 1098 (=1176 A.D.). Another record[22] of him at Drākshārāma is dated in 1177 A.D. refers to his name as Narēndradēva, and the son of Vijayādityadēva. It is of interest to note a record of the Kākatīya king Rudradēva Rāju, as Drākshārāma dated in S' 1108 (=1186 A.D.) which registers a gift of lamp.[23] In this grant reference is not made to the reigning Chāḷukya-Chōḷa king or to his regnal years but to one *Sarvalokāśraya Viṣṇuvardhana Mahārāja* and his regnal years (the 5th year). It certainly fits into the reign of Vīranarēndra alias Viṣṇuvardhana *Chakravartin* of Bhimavaram and Drākshārāma records. The reasons for this may be related like this. The effective rule of the Chāḷukya-Chōlas in Coastal Andhra districts ended with the reign of Rājarāja II, i.e., 1173 A.D. Because of the desire of the Kākatīyas to occupy the Coastal Andhra tract few battles were waged and in one of them Prōla II was dead.[24] His son, Rudradēva's[25] records dated A.D. 1158, 1168 and 1186 are noted at Drakshārāma. Of these, the first two[26] are dated in the regnal years of Rājarāja II. There was a political vacuum in Āndhradēśa after the reign of Rājarāja II till the establishment of a local dynasty by Rājādhirāja II[27] of the Chāḷukya-Chōḷa line of kings whose records are found at Drākshārāma 1193 A.D.[28] Hence, it may be pointed out that because of this, the Kākatīya ruler Rudradēva mentioned the regnal years of Viṣṇuvardhana Mahārāja (alias Vīranarēndra) in his Drākshārāma record. The latest record of this Viṣṇuvardhana at Juttiga is dated in 1187 A.D., which shows that he reigned upto the year 1187 A.D. Belonging to the same family, Mallapadēva Bhūpati, son of Vijayāditya III by Gaṇgādēvī alias Viṣṇu-vardhana Mahārāja ascended the throne at Piṭhāpuram in the Śaka year 1124 (=1202 A.D.).[30] A record of him is found at Bhimavaram.[31]

Inscriptions at Palivela,[32] Razole taluk in Godavari District reveal the existence of two more Viṣṇuvardhana Mahārājas in this century. They were Ballahadēva Chakravartin and his son Bhīmadēva Chakravartin. Ballahādēva's accession is calculated as 1177 A.D. and his latest record[33] is dated in 1179 A.D. It seems that his son reigned for 10 years i.e., from A.D. 1192 to 1202 A.D., whose record is also noticed at Sarpavaram.[34] We do not know for certain to which family these two Viṣṇuvardhanas belong.

The genealogy and chronology of the Viṣṇuvardhana Mahārājas of 12th Century A.D. may be formulated as follows :

Vijayāditya (III) A.D. 1126/27—1148 A.D.

Mallapadēva Chakravartin A.D. 1173/74-1183 A.D.	Vīranarēndra A.D. 1179/80-1187	Mallapadēva Bhūpati A.D. 1202

O

O

O

O

Ballahadēva Chakravartin A.D. 1177—1179 A.D.

()

()

Bhīmadēva Chakravartin A.D. 1192—1202 A.D.

The foregoing study reveals the existence of 6 Viṣṇuvardhana Mahārājas in 12th Century A.D. apart from the Chaḷukya-Chōḷa kings. Of them 4 kings may be identified with the kings of the minor Chāḷukyan family that established in the vicinity of Piṭhāpuram. Their rule was mentioned optionally by the people of the time. Feeble or effective their rule covered a period of one century. From 13th Century onwards the Viṣṇuvardhana Mahārājas of the period are invariably referred to in the records with their personal names. Thus the names of the several kings of Chāḷukyas of Niḍadavole, Elamanchili and Piṭhāpuram appear in the inscriptions along with the usual epithet, *Viṣṇuvardhana Mahārāja.* It has also been shown above that the Viṣṇuvardhana Mahārājas of the records of the 12th Century A.D. has nothing to do with reigning Chāḷukyā chōla kings after Kulōttuṅga I. It is significant to state here that unlike the several *māṇḍalikas* such as Velanāti Chōlas and Haihayas of Kōna and others, these Viṣṇuvardhana Mahārājas under study have issued their records independently without referring to the name or the regnal years of the reigning Chāḷukya-Chōlas.

NOTES AND REFERENCES

1. *S.I.I.*, Vol. IV, Nos. 1337, 1187, 1248, 1262, 1266.
2. Dr. N. Venkataramanaiah, *The Eastern Chālukyaṣ of Vengī*, Appendix I, pp. 295-302.
3. *S.I.I.*, Vol. IV Nos. 1280, 1112, 1113, 1107, 1104, 1102 ; *S.I.I.*, Vol. VI, Nos. 123, 129, 135, 147, 150, 172, 175.
4. *Ep. Ind.*, Vol. VI, No. 35.
   Ep. Ind., Vol. V, No. 10.
   S.I.I., Vol. I, No. 39.
5. The identification of the place Jananāthapuri is still a controversial matter. Some identified it with Drākshārāma and the others with Rajahmundry.
6. *Bharati*, 1968, June.
7. *Ep. Ind.*, Vol. IV, No. 33.
8. *S.I.I.*, Vol. VI, No. 123 ; *Ep. Ind.*, Vol. IV, No. III, p. 225. A.R.E., 102 of 1922.
9. *Ibid.*, Vol. IV, Nos. 1170, 1176, 1177, 1191, 1192, 1193, 1195, 1196, 1197, and 1198.
10. *Ibid.*, Nos. 1191, 1192, 1195, 1196, 1197, 1198.
11. *Ibid.*, No. 1193.
12. *Ibid.*, No. 1177.
13. *Ibid* , 1170.
14. *Bharati*, 1968 January.
15. *Ep. Ind.*, Vol. IV, No. 33.
16. *Ep. Ind.*, Vol. IV, No. III, p. 225.
17. *S.I.I.*, Vol. X, No. 110, 116, 11, 12. It is of interest to note that there is a reference to *Dākarēmi Nandi Mānika* a measure of ghee named after the place Ḍakarēmi (=Drākshārāma in his record at Juttiga). This would support the assumption that Dākarēmi or Drākshārāma was under the sway of the Chāḷukyas of Piṭhāpuram.
18. *S.I I.*, Vol. X, No. 116.
19. *Ibid.*, V, Nos. 77, 91, 90, 89, 67.
20. *Ibid.*, No. 67.
21. *Ibid.*, No. 61.
22. *Ibid.*, Vol. IV, No. 1373-A.
23. *Ibid.*, No. 1155.
24. *Ibid*,, No. 1242.
25. *Ibid.*, Nos. 1095, 1107, 1155.
26. *Ibid.*, 1095, 1107.
27. *Itihas*, Vol. IX and X, 1982, pp. 1-4.
28. *S.I.I.*, Vol. IV, No. 1223.
29. *Ibid.*, Vol. X, No. 203.
30. *Ep. Ind.*, Vol. IV, No. 33, p. 228.
31. *S,I.I.*, Vol. V, No. 93.
32. *Ibid.*, No. 111, 112.
33. *Ibid.*, Vol. IV, No. 1261.
34. *Ibid.*, V, No. 8.

9

TAMIL INFLUENCE ON PERSONAL AND PLACE NAMES IN THE COASTAL DISTRICTS OF MEDIEVAL ANDHRA

During the 11th and 12th centuries A.D. Andhra was under the rule of the Chāḷukya-Chōḷas, who exercised their power from Tanjore. After the death of the Eastern Chāḷukyan king, Vijayāditya VII in 1076 A.D. Kulōttuṅga I, the first Chāḷukya-Chōḷa ruler governed Āndhradēśa by appointing his sons as viceroys of Vēṅgī. The fusion of the two crowns—the Eastern Chāḷukyan and the Chōḷa into one as the Chāḷukya-Chōḷa had resulted in the extension of the power of the Chōḷas in Andhra. Several permanent trails such as monuments, inscriptions, coins, literary works and places names had been left behind as a result of this. In the present paper, an attempt is made to trace the Tamil influence on the personal and place names in the coastal districts of Andhra region of the medieval times, on the basis of the Telugu and Tamil inscriptions in Āndhradēśa. I have also attempted to trace the origin of some of the present day place-names, in the light of the available historical information.

It was a common practice in the Tamil land to refer to *brahmādēyas as chaturvēdimangalams*[1] which were associated with the names of either the donor or the reigning kings, but, this was not so, in the case of the Andhra region. In Andhra, they are called only as the *agrahāra* villages and not named after either the donor or the ruling king. The Piṭhāpuram copper plate inscription of Vīrachōḍa[2] (dated, A.D. 1093) informs that the village Ālavelli with its 12 hamlets and Ponnatoṟṟa, both in Prōlunāḍu *vishaya* and Ālami in Uttarāvarusa *vishaya* were united and renamed as Virachōḍa *chaturvēdimangalam* after the name of the viceroy of Vēṅgi, Vīrachōḍa. This record can be considered the earliest inscription in Andhra to refer to the existence of a a *chaturvēdimangalam* in the coastal Andhra region. Few inscriptions at Drākshārāma[3] and Sarpavaram[4] datable to the reign-period of Kulōttuṅga I mention Rājēndrachōda *chaturvedimangalam* and Chuttamalli *chaturvēdimangalam*. Rājendrachōḍa was the princely name of Kulōttuṅga I after whom the village had been named. This includes certain portions of the present Kakinada and Piṭhāpuram Taluks of East Godavari districts. The significance of the term Chuttamalli prefixed to the *chaturvēdimangalam* is not clear. However, from the provenance of the stone inscriptions of the area, it can be assumed that it includes portions of Kakinada Taluk.

In the same manner, the villages endowed to the learned brahmins were also termed as 'nallūr' along with the name or title of the donor in the Tamil region, which was also a new practice in the Andhra region. It is clear from the epigraphic evidence that Kalidiṇḍi in Krishna District was renamed as Madhurāntaka Chōḷa nallūr, probably after the title of Rājēndra Chōḷa (A.D. 1012—1044).

During this period, some important religious and trade centres were renamed after the names of the Chōḷa kings or their titles. Bezawāda (Vijayawada) was referred to as Rājēndra Chōḷāpuram after the princely name of Kulōttuṇga I in a Tamil inscription[5] of the same place. After the title of the king, Rājarāja II, Prēmpalli (Bapatla in Guntur district) was named as Rājamāṇikkavuram.[6] Visakhapatnam, an important trade centre, was rechristened as Kulōttuṇgachōḍa paṭṭaṇam[7] after the name of Kulōttuṅga I. Likewise, several villages and towns in Andhra were renamed after the reigning Chōḷa rulers of the period, as they were the overlords of the entire Andhra region and also probably to commemorate their successful military conquests. However, it appears that these new names did not become much popular as these new names are mentioned in very few inscriptions in the succeeding periods.

The village Jananāthapura[8] is mentioned in the copper plate grants and the stone inscriptions as the capital city of the Chāḷukya-Choḷa rulers in Andhra and as situated on the banks of the river Gōdāvarī. It was probably named after the title 'Jananātha' of the Chōḷa king Rājarāja I (A.D. 985-1016). It has been identified with Drākshārāma by some scholars,[9] but this identification is questionable.[10] Today, in the East and West Godavari districts, several villages are known with the name of Jagannathapuram, probably a variant of Jananāthapura.

Villages with the names of Chodavaram in East Godavari district and Visakhapatnam district could have been so named after the Chōḷas who extended their rule into Andhra during the medieval times. Similarly, the present-day place-names like Aravaplli,[11] Arepalle, and Arepalle *agrahāram*[12] could have derived their names after the people, *aravas* i.e., the Tamil speaking people, who settled in that area. This shows that certain villages, inhabited by the people of the Tamil country were named after either the ruling dynasty or after the language they spoke.

The entire Andhra region was named after Kulōttuṅga I as Kulottuṅga-chōlamaṇḍalam[13] under the rule of the Chāḷukya-Chōḷas. Kulōttuṅga I, started a new administrative division called 'valanāḍu' during his reign-period for the sake of revenue administration. As Anndhra region formed a part of the Chōḷa empire, it was also divided into various 'valanāḍu' divisions which were named after the epithets of Kulōttuṅga I. Similarly, Gangagoṇḍa-chōḍa valanāḍu[12] comprising parts of East and West Godavari districts seems to have been named after the epithet of Rājēndra I (A.D. 1012-44), 'Gangayum Gaḍāramumgoṇḍa.' Jayagoṇṇaśōla maṇḍalam[16] was named after the epithet, 'Jayagoṇḍaśōḷa' of the Chōḷa king Rājarāja I (A.D. 985-1016), comprising the southern parts of Andhra Pradesh and also parts of Tamilnadu.

Under the rule of the Chāḷukya-Chōḷas, a number of generals and chieftains have been elevated of their status to that of the *mahāmaṇḍalēsvaras* because of their meritorious military services and the help they rendered to their overlords. Some of the *māṇḍalika* chiefs had also prefixed to their personal names, the names of the Chāḷukya-Chōḷa kings. The Velanāṭi chiefs—Gonka I, Chōḍa I, Gonka II, Rājēndrachōḍa II, Gonka III and Prithvīsvara prefixed the name 'Kulōttuṇga Chōḍa,' before their names.[17] This practice of prefixing the name of the sovereign suggest the unbounded devotion, and gratitude that the Valanatis had to their sovereign. Among the Haihaya chiefs of Kōnamaṇḍala, two rulers of the line bore the name, Rājēndra Chōḍa, which was the princely name of Kulōttuṅga I.[18]

The Piṭhāpuram plates of Vīrachōḍa refers to the names and *gotras* of a number of brahmins, as donees, of whom a majority of them were brought from the south (*dākshinātya dwijas*). The Mallavaram plates of Parāntaka[19] which registers the re-granting of the land shares to the remaining brahmins of the Vīrachōḍa *chaturvēdi mangalam* also mentions the names of the brahmins. Some of the names of the donees of the grant bear typical medieval Tamil names such as Karuṇākara, Aravinda, etc. This could have been due to the migration of a large number of Tamil brahmins as well as their settlement in the Andhra region during the time of Kulōttuṇga I.

Thus the above study reveals that several villages, towns and territorial divisions in Andhra were named after the names of the Chōḷa kings or their epithets during the medieval period. Although there is no reference and clues in the epigraphs of the period under consideration to the fact that the

Tamil speaking people had their own settlements in Andhra regions, this is apparent from the close study of the present day village names. The village names Aravapalli, Arepalli and Arepalli *agrahāram* adds significant evidence in this direction. Further, it is also made clear that the local chiefs of Andhra had also prefixed the names of the Chōḷa kings to their personal names. Thus due to the various factors such as political and socio-economic nature, the names of the persons as well as places have undergone changes through the centuries.

NOTES AND REFERENCES

1. *Ep. Ind.*, Vol. XXV, pp. 75-76.
2. *Ibid.*, Vol. V, No. 10.
3. *S.I.I.* Vol. IV, No. 1281.
4. *Ibid.*, Vol. V, Nos. 8, 12, 13, 15, 16.
5. *Ibid.*, Vol. No. 779.
6. *Ibid..* Vol. VI, No. 148.
7. *Ibid.*, Vol. X, No. 211, 251.
8. *Ep. Ind.*, Vol. V, No. 10 ; *S.I.I.*, Vol. I, No. 39 ; *Ep. Ind.*, Vol. VI, No. 35 ; N. Ramesan, *Studies in Medieval Deccan History* (Hyderabad, 1975), p. 81 ff ; *S.I.I.*, Vol. IV, No. 1384, 737.
9. K.A.N. Sastri, *The Cōlas* (Madras, 1955), p. 173 ; S.S. Ramachandra Murthy, *A Study of Telugu Place Names* (Delhi, 1985) p. 180.
10. In the stone inscriptions of Drākshārāma, it is mentioned variously as Drāchyārāma, Drākṣhārāma, Ḍākarēmi, Pedadākarēmi and Idai Karambai. And the place Jananātha-pura is mentioned in the copper-plate grants and few stone records of the Chālukya-Chōlas as well as in the records of the minor Chālukyan family of Pithapuram region. If both are identical, it could have been referred to in the inscriptions. For more details See K, Suryanaryana, *Minor Chālukyan Families in Medieval Āndhradēśa* (Delhi, 1986), pp. 73-117.
11. Aravapalli is located at a distance of 3 km. from Repalle in Guntur District.
12. It is located in Narasaraopet taluk of Guntur District.
13. *S.I.I.*, Vol. V, No. 66 ; *Ibid.*, Vol. VI, No. 200.
14. S.S. Ramachandra Murthy, *op. cit.*, p. 146.
15. *S.I.I.* Vol. V, No. 66.
16. S.S. Ramachandra Murty, *op. cit.*, pp. 68, 69.
17. B.V. Krishna Rao, *History of the Eastern Chālukyas of Vēṅgī*, (Hyderabad, 1973), p. 445; *Ep. Ind.* Vol. XXIX, No. 32.
18. *S.I.I.*, Vol. IV, No. 1150 ; M. Krishna Kumari, *The Rule of the Chālukya-Cholas in Āndhradēsa*, p. 250.
19. N. Ramesan, *op. cit.*, pp. 81 ff.

10

LAMP GRANTS IN THE DRĀKSHĀRĀMA TEMPLE

Drākshārāma is 9 kms. away from the village of Kotipalli on the banks of the river Gautamī, the main branch of the river Gōdāvary, which branched off into seven branches from the beginning of its delta at Rajahmundry. It is one of the famous *pañchārāmas*, the remaining four being Amarārāma, Kshīrārāma, Kumārārāma and Bhīmarama. The presiding deity of the Drākshārāma temple is lord Bhīmēsvara. In the inscriptions of the temple, the place is mentioned as Drāchyārāma, Dākarēmi and Pedaḍākarēmi.[1]

The main theme of this paper is to study the lamp grants of the temple in detail and to compare them with the lamp grants of the remaining four *ārāmas*, as it provides an insight into the economic conditions of medieval Āndhradēśa. Out of the 375 records of the temple so far noticed, 236 of them were registering the lamp grants. They cover a long period of time, i.e., from the first part of 11th Century A.D. to 14th Century A.D., thus covering a period of nearly four centuries time. The temple enjoyed the patronage of the Eastern Chāḷukyas of Vēṅgī, the Chāḷukya-Chōḷas, the Chāḷukyas of Kalyāṇi, Eastern Gāṅgas, the Kākatīyas, Reḍḍis and several *maṇḍalika* Chieftains of Āndhradēśa.

Though the Drākshārāma temple enjoyed the patronage of several major powers in the long span of time, maximum number of lamp donations were made in the 1st half of 12th Century A.D. (i.e., between A.D. 1100 and A.D. 1150). It appears from the records that setting up of perpetual lamps was the most favoured service among the people of middle ages. Out of the 236 inscriptions mentioning the gift of lamps, 139 records were issued between A.D. 1101 and A.D. 1150. The following table would show that the setting-up of perpetual lamps had come down gradually in the subsequent period.

TABLE 1

Lamp Grants in the Drākshārāma Temple

	1000-1050 A.D.	1051-1100 A.D.	1101-1150 A.D.	1151-1200 A.D.	1201-1250 A.D.	1251-1300 A.D.	1301-1350 A.D.	Total No. of Inscriptions
Number of inscriptions registering lamp grants	1	10	139	53	18	14	1	236

From the records of Drākshārāma temple it is clear that the devotee had to donate either 55 or 50 cows to set up one *akhanḍadīpā* and 25 cows for the up-keep of *aradivya* (1/2 lamp). The cows thus donated were kept incharge of a headman of the *bōya* family under a trust committee of four or six elders of the *bōya* family. The names of the trustee and the cowherds are mentioned in the inscriptions. In turn, the cowherds had to provide 1 *tribhuvanāṁkuśa māna* of ghee for the burning of the perpetual lamp, daily, as long as the sun and the moon survive. A study of the Drākshārāma inscriptions show that on the occasions such as *Uttarāyaṇa saṁkrānti*,[2] *Kanyāsaṁkrānti*,[3] *Karkāṭaka saṁkrānti*,[4] *Vishuvu saṁkrānti*,[5] *Dakshiṇayaṇa Saṁkrānti*,[6] Solar eclipse,[7] *Vyatīpātamu*,[8] *Mahādvādasi*,[9] and *Tulāsaṁkrānti*[10] the lamp grants were made by the people. In addition to these auspicious occasions gift of lamps were also made by the *mānḍalikas* and the military chiefs after their successful military conquests[11] or for the merit of their parents,[12] son,[13] wife,[14] king[15] and friends[16] or for their own religious merit.[17] The common expression found in the temple records for the milk yielding animals is *inupa yeḍlu*,[18] *enupa yeḍlu*,[19] *enumulu*,[20] *modavulu* or *mōdālu*[21] and *surabhulu*.[22] Some records refer to the gift of 25 cows for keeping the perpetual lamp, which would fetch one *tribhuvanāṁkuśa māna* of ghee. It is of interest to notice a record which refer to the gift of cows of as many as 425 for the upkeep of a lamp in the temple.[23] Not merely the cows were gifted for the upkeep of the lamps but sometimes the land was also gifted to maintain the lamps in the temple.[24] Lands and house sites were gifted for the cowherds, who were looking after the maintenance of the lamp grant.[25] Very rarely, money was also gifted for keeping the lamp in the temple. In an inscription it is stated that 10 Kulôttuṅga *māḍas* are given for setting up a lamp.[26] In another record it is mentioned that 10 Kulōttuṅga *gadyas* are given to the temple for the upkeep of a lamp.[27]

In the Drākshārāma inscriptions it is stated that the cows gifted to the lord are placed incharge of one or more reliable cowherds under a trust committee of four or six elders.[28] The donors of the lamp-grant took a great care for the safety and longevity of their grants. For this purpose, the donated cows were kept incharge of (*aḍapuna*) certain *boyas,* who might have been the head officers. Important of them were Talarāsi, Talarāsi Nāvaya, Modali, etc.[29] The cows thus gifted were placed in the cattlepens of the cowherds or in that of the temple. The following table will show clearly the details relating to the number of cows gifted and the cattlepens referred to in the inscriptions in different periods.

TABLE 2

	1000-1050 A.D.	1051-1100 A.D.	1101-1150 A.D.	1151-1200 A.D.	1201-1250 A.D.	1251-1300 A.D.	1301-1350 A.D.	Total
Number of cows mentioned	—	775	5,735	1,605	620	250	—	8,985
Number of ins-criptions mention-ing cattle-pens (*Vasams*)	—	9	79	23	2	4	1	118

A glance at the above table shows that a large number of cows, i.e., 5,735 were donated between 1101 and 1150 A.D. Subsequently, the number of cows donated decreases gradually. It is also the same as regards to the reference to the number of various cattle pens (*Vasamulu*) mentioned in the records. A large number of records (i.e., 79) mentioned the cattle pens in the same period and its number has drastically come down to one in the period between 1301 and 1350 A.D.

Quite interestingly, the records of Drākshārāma mentioned the practice of keeping the lamps burning in the temple twice (*renḍavu naḍapuna*) thrice (*mūṇḍavu naḍapuna*) and four times (*nālgavu naḍpuna*) daily. This practice is not to be found anywhere in the records of the temples of Āndhradēśa. The details relating this practice are shown in the table given below.

TABLE—3

	1000-1050 A.D.	1050-1100 A.D.	1101-1150 A.D.	1151-1200 A.D.	1201-1250 A.D.	1251-1300 A.D.	1301-1350 A.D.	Total No. of records
Number of records mentioning the burning of the lamps twice daily (*reṇḍavu naḍapuna*)	—	—	15	11	5	—	—	31
Number of records mentioning the burning of the lamps thrice daily (*mūṇḍavu naḍapuna*)	—	—	13	11	3	—	—	27
Number of records mentioning the burning of the lamps four times daily (*nālgavu-naḍpuna*)	—	—	2	6	2	—	—	10

It is obvious from the above table, that the practice of making specifications as regards to burning of the lamps in the temple are carefully registered in the lamp grants of 12th Century A.D. It also indicates that the people of the time had favoured much to keep the lamps burning twice daily in the temple. Next in preference comes the lighting of the lamps three times daily.

In the remaining four *ārāmas* the lamp grants were not as many as in the Drākhsārāma temple. For example, in the Sōmārāmam temple at

Guṇupūḍi Bhīmavaram, there are only two records so far noticed.[30] In the Kshīrārāmēsvara temple at Palakollu, out of the 46 inscriptions of the temple, 27 of them registers lamp grants.[31] In the Chāḷukya Bhīmēsvara temple at Bhīmavaram, out of the 64 inscriptions of the temple, only 17 records were the lamp grants. In the Drākshārāma records, *tribhuvanāṁkuśa māna* is mentioned as the measurement for the ghee, whereas in the Bhīmavaram records *Sāniyaṁbāṭi mānika* and *Rājamāna mānika* are mentioned.[32] Unlike the Drākshārāma temple records, the Kshīrārāmēsvara records refer *Nandi mānika*[33] as the measure and the lamp grants were entrusted to the temple superintendent or to the *Sāni munnūrvuru guild*.[34]

Thus the study of the lamp grants in the Drākshārāma temple provide us the information about the system of gifting the perpetual lamps to the temples during the medieval times. For the reasons unknown, at the present state of our knowledge, the lamp grants made in the Drakshārāma temple were numerous in the 1st half of 12th Century A.D. and the same was the case in the temples of Amarāvati and Bhīmavarm. But interestingly, in the Kshīrārāmēsvara temple at Pālakollu, the maximum number of perpetual lamps were set up during the 13th Century A.D. and the number had come down drastically in the subsequent periods.[35] Thus the present study gives us a clear idea about the economic conditions of the five Śaivite temples in medieval Āndhradēśa and their patronage during the different periods.

NOTES AND REFERENCES

1. *S.I.I.* Vol. IV, Nos. 949, 1102, 1104, 1108, 1228.
2. *Ibid.*, Nos. 1156, 1170, 1177, 1201.
3. *Ibid.*, No. 1013.
4. *Ibid.*
5. *Ibid.*, Nos. 1132, 1165, 1266, 1086, 1091.
6. *Ibid.*, Nos. 1233, 1094, 1113.
7. *Ibid.*, Nos. 1112, 1171, 1025.
8. *Ibid.*, Nos. 1167, 1191, 1194, 1195.
9. *Ibid.*, Nos. 1032-A.
10. *Ibid.*, Nos. 1300, 1305, 1365.
11. *Ibid.*, Nos. 1083, 1117.
12. *Ibid.*, Nos. 1117, 1279, 1100, 1078.
13. *Ibid.*, No. 1068.
14. *Ibid.*, No. 1335.
15. *Ibid.*, Nos. 1152, 1342.
16. *Ibid.*, No. 1228.
17. *Ibid.*, Nos. 1145, 1212, 1215, 1244.

18. *Ibid.*, Nos. 1013, 1158.
19. *Ibid.*, Nos. 1008, 1011, 1010,
20. *Ibid.*, No. 1187.
21. *Ibid.*, Nos. 1138, 1163, 1217, 1235.
22. *Ibid.*, Nos. 1288, 1290.
23. *Ibid.* No. 1140.
24. *Ibid.*, Nos. 1068, 1203.
25. *Ibid.*, Nos. 1080, 1083.
26. *Ibid.*, Nos. 1063.
27. *Ibid.*, No. 1051.
28. *Ibid.*, Nos. 1045, 1018, 1035, 1014.
29. *Ibid.*, Nos. 1018, 1020, 1073, 1208, 1049, 1135, 1143, 1144.
30. *Annual Report on South Indian Epigraphy for 1943-45*. Nos. 4 and 5 ; Also see *J.A.H.R.S.* Vol. XXI, pp. 95-99.
31. *Jounral of Epigraphical Society of India*, 1981, pp. 105-108.
32. *S.I.I.* Vol. V, Nos. 63, 67, 71, 72, 73, 74.
33. *Ibid.*, Nos. 121, 122, 127.
34. *Ibid.*, Nos. 160, 161, 162.
35. *Journal of Epigraphical Society of India*, 1981, pp. 105-108.

11

A NOTE ON THE VILLAGE GRANTS IN ANDHRA UNDER THE RULE OF THE CHĀḶUKYA-CHŌLAS

Several inscriptions in Andhra record the village donations made to the brahmins, temples and to the institutions attached to the temples such as *maṭhas, satrams,* etc. As the villages and towns were under the suzerainty of a king, he alone could grant the villages or towns for the charitable purposes. However, the royal princes or the heir-apparents were also authorized to exercise the royal privilege of granting the villages. Further, a cursory glance at the epigraphic evidence of the period shows that a considerable number of villages were donated by the *māṇḍalikas* to the important religious institutions of the period, i.e., the temples, which emerged as the legitimisers of political power and as an instrument of peasant subordination and surplus accumulation.[1] It appears that the feudatories of varying rank and power had liberally patronised the temple institutions by giving away the land and village donations to stabilise their political power in the state. An attempt is made here to study the nature of the village grants in Andhra and the state of the king in the revenue system during the 11th and 12th centuries A.D.

The copper plate grants[2] of the sons of Kulōttuṅga I issued in Andhra allude to the donation of the three villages along with several hamlets, which was named as Vīrachōḍa *chaturvēdī mangalam*, to a large number of brahmins. A close perusal of the names of the donees listed in the Pithapuram and Mallavaram plates indicate that most of them hail from the Tamil land.[3] Besides this *brahmādēya* settlement, the stone inscriptions of the reign-period of Kulōttuṅga I reveal the existence of Rājēndrachōda *chaturvēdi mangalam* and Chuttamalli *chaturvēdi mangalam* in Andhra.[4] These *brahmādēya* lands were exempted from the payment of all kinds of taxes, i.e., *sarvakaraparihāra*.[5]

Not only the *brahmādēya* villages but also the villages donated to the temples, i.e., *dēvadāna* lands were exempted from the taxes. Great care had been taken to mention in the inscriptions whether, or not, the grant was free of all taxes and other payments, so that there would be no confusion at the time of collecting the revenues and taxes by the officials of the state. The villages exempted from taxes are known in the inscriptions as *iraiyili* or *iraiyili dēvadāna*. Inscriptions and Drākshārāma show that the villages donated by the kings to the temples were exempted from the taxes. In such cases, the inscriptions were attested by the names of the royal officials. For instance, an inscription[6] dated in the 49th regnal year of Kulōttuṅga I registers the gifts of the village Īyūru along with its boundaries and waste lands to Parāntakēsvara Mahādēva. It also states that the land taxes like *pannasamu*, *antarāyamu* and *kīḍera* were all exempted by the king. The minister of war and peace, Rājamanōhara Brahma mārāyar and Sāvanna-dirāyar, another official seems to have granted the exemption of taxes on the *devadāna* village. Since the king made the *iraiyili* grant from the proceeds of the state to the temple the income of the state in the form of the taxes is now transferred to the temple treasury.[7] Probably, for this reason, the royal officials appear in the records to administer the accounts as the king is releasing the state funds. In another instance,[8] Rājarāja II had granted the villages to Pāka alla alamu and Boyi Velumapalli as *sarvakara parihāra* to feed the ascetics in the *satram* established by him. In this inscription also, the names and signatures of the royal officers, i.e., the *peggadas* and *daṇḍanāyakas* are mentioned.

From the epigraphic evidence of the period it appears that it was absolutely necessary for the officials, *mānḍalikas* and others to obtain prior permission from the reigning king before making the village grants.[9] This can be attested to by the mentioning of the name of the reigning Chālukya-Choḷa king and his regnal years in their records. Unlike the village grants[10] issued by the kings and the heir-apparents, which were attested by the signatures and names of the royal officials, the village grants of the *māndalikas* and the officials were devoid of such things. In certain cases, when the land was donated by an official the tax exemption was granted by the local assembly, i.e., the *mahājanas*. It is stated in an inscription at Drākshārāma[11] that Mūvēnda Vēlān paid some gold (*pahiṁḍi*) to the *Mahājanas* of Rājēndrachoḍa *Chaturvedi mangalam* in whose jurisdiction had been located the donated village, to exempt it from the payment of taxes. Since this organisation is entrusted with the function of collecting the land dues in the administration, it was permitted to give the tax exemptions. As there is no reference in the grant to the royal officials, it can be said that the *mahajana* organisation is independent of the government and it need not take formal approval of the state. From this it can be inferred that the royal officers appear in the records for administrative purpose to record the loss of revenue to the state when the land was granted tax-free by the kings and heir-apparents. When the *mahājana* organisation is making a tax-free grant by receiving a certain amount of gold from the donor, it should be understood, that the taxes were not really exempted. In other words, the amount of gold received was loaned and the interest was treated as equivalent to tax demand. Hence, in this instance, as there is no loss to the state revenue, the royal officials do not figure, since they have no administrative duty to perform. Though a considerable number of *dēvadāna* donations were made by the *māṇdalikas*, it has not been stated in the records that they were exempted from the payment of taxes.

It is clear from the records under study that the main purpose of the *dēvadāna* grants, which carries with them the eight kinds of enjoyment, (*aṣṭa bhōga salvi saṁpadalu*)[13] was to ensure the permanency of the services for which they were granted. The perpetual nature of the village grants which may either be the *agrahāra* or *dēvadāna* donations had been emphasized by the frequent occurrence of imprecatory verses at the end of the records. These grants provided the permanent source of income to the temples to conduct *havi, bali,* and *archana*[14] to conduct the festivals[15] for maintaining *anga ronga bhōgas*[16] for *chandana* and *karpūra naivedyam*[17] and to feed the brahmins and ascetics[18] coming from the distant lands and residing in the institutions attached to the temples. It has also been stipulated in some of the epigraphs at the time of donating the villages to the temples, that these grants should be maintained by the *sthānapati, devakarmins* and *sānulu-mānulu.*[19] Further it is also specifically mentioned in some records of Drākshārmā that provision should be made out of the donated villages to provide lands to the various temple functionaries in lieu of their services.[20]

The several stone and copper-plate grants registering the village endowments distributed in various parts of Andhra have been arranged in the following table basing on the actual nature of the grants.

Sl. No.	Nature of the endowments	Number of the records
1.	Villages donated to the brahmins	8
2.	Villages donated to the temples	16
3.	Rulership of *raḍḍikam* conferred on the chiefs	2
4.	Villages donated to the *satrams* attached to the temples	4
	Total:	30

From the above table, it is clear that out of the 30 gifts of villages, 16 were made to the temples as *dēvadāna* and only 8 were made to the brahmins as *agrahara* villages. It has been observed by Prof. Burton Stein[21] that there is a decline in the patronage of *brahmādēyas* in the Tamil region after the time of Kulōttuṅga I. This is corroborated by the present analysis of the village endowments in Andhra, as a majority of the village grants were made to the temples than to the brahmins. It appears from the present survey of the epigraphic sources that the temple lands had been enormously increased leading to an expansion of the temple personnel, who were paid through allotments of some shares in the temple lands. To get a clear idea about the donors of these village endowments the inscriptional data is arranged in the following table.

Sl. No.	Donor	No. of Records
1.	Kings	4
2.	Viceroys	5
3.	*Maṇḍalikas*	17
4.	Ministers	3
5.	Others	1
	Total :	30

The above table shows that, out of the 30 village grants, the *maṅḍalikas* had donated a large number of them, i.e., 17, whereas the kings had granted only 4 and the viceroys 5, village grants. Though efforts have been made by Kulōttuṅga I during his reign-period to strengthen the central authority by establishing several hundreds of Tamil brahmins near his capital city in Andhra, Jananāthapura, by liberally donating the villages to them, such kind of efforts were not made by his successors. It is apparent from the present study that the period witnessed the increasing power of the feudatory chiefs, which is reflected in the issueing of a large number of *dēvadāna* grants by them than the kings. It also highlights the deep faith of feudal lords in promoting the temples as well as the other institutions such as *maṭhas* and *satrams*, which caters the needs of the students, ascetics and brahmins coming from the far off places. From the examination of the process of the tax exemptions made by the king in making the *dēvadāna* as well as the *agrahāra* villages, the royal privileges and his state in the revenue system could be indicated.

NOTES AND REFERENCES

1. R.N. Nandi, "Growth of Rural Economy in Early Feudal India", Presidential address, Ancient India (Section I), Proceedings of the Forty-Fifth Session, *Indian History Congress*, Annamalainagar, 1984, pp. 25-91 ; Idem., "Feudalization of the State in Medieval South India," *Social Science Probings*, Vol. I, No. 1, March, 1984, pp. 33-59.
2. *A.P.A.R.E.* Cp. No. 1 of 1965 ; N. Ramesan, *Studies in Medieval Deccan* pp. 110 ff. *Ep. Ind, Vol.* V, No. 10.
3. *Ibid.*
4. *S.I.I.*, Vol. IV, No. 1281.
5. When a village was endowed and stated to be tax-free (*sarva kara parihōra*), it did not mean that the village or the inhabitants were freed from the payment of taxes but what it meant was that, the income, which till the time of the grant replenished the treasury of the king ceased to go to him but was diverted to the donee or religious institutions specified in the grant. See for more details, C. Minakshi, *Administration and Social Life under the Pallavas*, University of Madras, 1977, pp. 88.
6. *S.I.I.*, Vol. VI, No. 1226.
7. P. Shanmugam, "Tax Free Grants during Rājarāja I", Proceedings of the 45th Session of *Indian History Congress*, 1984, pp. 177-182.
8. *S.I.I.*, Vol. IV, No. 1102.
9. *Ibid.*, 1248, 1281, 1288, 1104, 1371.
10. *Ibid.*, Nos. 1226, 1102 ; *A.P.A.R.E.*, Ch. No. 1 of 1965, *Ep. Ind.*, Vol. V, No. 10.
11. *S I.I.*, Vol. IV, No. 1281.
12. *Ibid.*, Nos. 795, Vol. VI, Nos. 121, 124, 610, 624 ; Vol. X, 242.
13. *Ibid.*, Vol. IV, Nos. 1281, 1371, 1288.
14. *Ibid.*, Vol. VI, Nos. 610, Vol. IV, Nos. 795, 1286.
15. *S.I.I.* Vol. VI, No. 121 ; Vol. IV, No. 1043, 1368, 1373.
16. *Ibid.*, Vol. X, No. 241.
17. *Ibid.*, Vol. IV, No. 1186, 1291.
18. *Ibid.*, Vol. IV, No. 1288, 1281, 1248, 1102, 1104.
19. *Ibid.*, Vol. IV, No. 155, 610.
20. *Ibid.*, Vol. IV, No. 1288, 1248.
21. Burton Stein, *Peasant State and Society in Medieval South India*, (Oxford University Press, 1980), p. 243.

12

LAND TRANSACTIONS AS SEEN IN THE DRAKSHARAMA INSCRIPTIONS

In the present paper it is proposed to study the land grants of Drākshārāma temple with the application of the statistical methods and to examine the developments or changes in land-holding as well as the administration of Andhra under the Chāḷukya-Chōḷas. Though similar type of studies have been made previously by scholars like Profs. Noboru Karashima, Burton, Stein, Subbarayalu, Sri Tirumalai and others they have mainly concentrated on the Tamil records of Chōḷa homeland. An effort is made here with the view that the systematic application of statistical methods to the land grants of Āndhradēśa which had been annexed to the Chōḷa state since the reign-period of Kulōttuṅga I, would settle some of the problems and theories posed by the historians. For this purpose, I have taken up the study of the inscriptions of Drākshārāma temple, where one finds a large number of land grants of the time of the Chāḷukya-Chōḷas.

There are approximately 379 published inscriptions of the temple, out of which 53 epigraphs records the land sale, donation of land taxes, land or village donation to the temple or to the *maṭhas* and choultries attached to the temple. Considering the status of the donors, the records are arranged in the table, which explains clearly that a maximum number (45.16%) of land donations were made by the ministers, officers and the servants of the *māṇḍalikas* rather than the *māṇḍalika* chiefs (16.13%) and the viceroys (9.69%) in the first half of 12th Century A.D. Of the land grants issued by the category of officers, ministers and servants in the long range of period a maximum number (77.77%) of the land donations were made in the period between 1101 A.D. and 1150 A.D. out of the 18 land donations were made by the 'others' i.e., private individuals are also amounting a large number (72.72%) out of the 11 grants made by them. A close study of these epigraphs reveal that they are mostly the land grants donated by the people from neighbouring regions like Vīragoṭṭam, Chakragoṭṭam and the Tamil region.[1] The presence of these people in this period in Andhra may be to strengthen and stabilize the Chāḷukya-Chōḷa power in Andhra as the period witnessed several political set-backs from the neighbouring regions. The table shows that the number of land grants decreased in the second half of 12th Century A.D. (22.22%) and were nil in the first half of 13th Century A.D. and only one grant in the first half of 14th Century A.D.

An analysis of the names and titles of the ministers reveals their status in the administration of the Chāḷukya-Chōḷa state. The frequent references[2] to the ministers having the titles such as *mūvēndavēlān pallavarāyar,* and *brahmamārāyar* either as donors of lands or as witnesses to them shows that they were working in the state administration and had the power to remit certain taxes due to the state, and to grant certain privileges. The evidence examined here supports the theory of Sri Noboru Karashima, who on the basis of the Tamil inscriptions of the Chōḷa state surmised that in the middle Chōḷa period which coincides with the reigns of Rājarāja I, Rājēndra I and Kulōttuṅga I, efforts were made by these kings to build up centralized administration.[3] The issuing of less number of land donations in the second half of 12th Century A.D. may be either due to the lessening of the Chōḷa interest in enforcing their imperial rule in the distant lands or as Andhra was frequently subjected to the invasions either from the side of the Chāḷukyas of Kalyāṇa or from the side of the Gāṅgas of Kaliṅga. Although the names of the Chōḷa rulers appear in the Andhra inscriptions continuously up to 1173 A.D. it shows only the formal acknowledgement of the suzerainty of the Chōḷas, as a majority of the records also appears without their names.

It is interesting to note that even the *māṇḍalikas* and the viceroys of Vēṅgī were making the land grants as *dēvadāna,* free of all taxes were attested by the signatures of the ministers.[4] This might be due to their power to collect the revenues from the lands gifted, of which some of them were generally exempted on their donations to the religious institutions. Some of the officials had their own land shares in certain villages. In 1278 A.D., a servant of the Kākatīya king Rudradēva gifted his share (*aṁdu mā pālu*) in the village Māmiṁḍivāḍa for the merit of the king.[5]

In the middle ages land became commodity, which was mostly desired as an article of gift. Possession of land also gave them a status in the society. It appears from the records under study, that land transfers took place between ministers, *māṇḍalikas* and private individuals or between

Table showing the number and percent land grants issued in different periods

Sl No.	Donors	A.D. 1050-1100	A.D. 1101-1150	A.D. 1151-1200	A.D. 1201-1250	A.D. 1251-1300	A.D. 1301-1350	Grand Total and %
				CENTURY				
1.	Officers, Ministers servants	1 (25.0)	14(77.7) (45.2)	2 (22.2)	—	1 (12.5)	—	18 (33.96)
2.	*Mahā-maṇḍalesvaras*	—	5(45.5) (16.1)	2 (22.2)	—	4 (50.0)	—	11 (20.75)
3.	King, Viceroys	2 (50.0)	3(60.0) (9.7)	—	—	—	—	5 (9.4)
4.	Ladies	1 (25.0)	1(12.5) (3.2)	3 (33.3)	—	3 (37.5)	—	18 (15.1)
5.	Others	—	8(72.7) (28.2)	2 (22.2)	—	—	1 (100.0)	11 (20. 7)
	Total	4 (7.5)	31 (58.5)	9 (16.98)	—	8 (15.1)	1 (1.9)	53 (100.0)

individuals and temples. Though it is registered in the records that the lands donated were purchased for the religious purpose just immediately before their donation, the evidence for secular transfer of land among individuals is not wanting. The wife of Anantapāla *Daṇḍānāyaka* purchased the garden land for 20 *Gandhahasti māḍas* and donated to the temple servants.[6] Saubhāgyadēva Rāja of Vīragoṭṭam granted 2 *puṭṭis* of land in Bikkavolu for offering *naivedyam* to the god.[7] It is stated in a record that Mallarāṇi of Chakragoṭṭam gave the land to Baliahuṇḍu which was enjoyed by the donor as his own, till it was donated.[8] The ministers of the time of Kulōttuṅga I having the titles *mūvēndavelān* purchased the villages from the *raṭṭoḍis*.[9]

Although all the lands were donated and not sold to the temple, we find some evidence of the existence of secular land transfer. The study of the lands adjoining the donated lands or villages reveals their connection with the personal names such as Somandari Pemmandari *tomṭa*, Prōle seṭṭi *tomṭa*, Kōna Bhīmarāju *tomṭa* and Erramanāyakuni *tomṭa*.[10] On the basis of this, it can be proposed that some of the garden lands were owned by private persons.

The Piṭhāpuram plates of Vīrachōḍa[11] registers the grant of Vīrachōḍa *Chaturvedimangalam* to 529 brahmins of the south by Vīrachōḍa. It is mentioned in the Mallavaram plates of Parāntaka Chōḷa that most of the brahmins whom Vīrachōḍa had brought and gave Vīrachōḍa *Chaturvedi mangalam* had left it, as they were unable to maintain themselves with the produce.[12] For this reason, Parāntaka Chōḻa regranted the entire village to 284 remaining brahmins. This shows that an *agrahāra* grant did not confirm the ownership of land but gave merely the title to income and produce of the land and the donor had the power to resume it, and regrant it or divide it into any other parts to suit to the convenience of the times.[13] But curiously, on contrary to this, it is stated in a record[14] that the village Āṇḍamūru being enjoyed by 8 brahmins, since they received it as a donation from Parāntaka Chōḻa, was sold to Ulaguyyavaṁda Pemmāḍi, the brother of Anantavarma Chōḍa Gaṅga for 120 *māḍas*. Further, another record[15] of Valavanmāttāṇḍa Mūvēnda Vēlān states that he purchased the land in the village of Ālavelli in Vīra Chōḍa *Chaturvedi mangalam* by giving gold. In this regard, it is stated that the people of Ālavelli should take the responsibility for cultivation of the land (*Ālavelli vāre ī bhūmi krushi sesi*) and they have to feed 20 brahmins by its produce. In the same record, it is stated that the 102 *mahājanas* of the disturbed village of Rājēndra Chōḍa of Sakaṭamantani nāḍu had sold 20 *puṭṭis* of land and agreed to the condition that the land is to be cultivated by the people of the village (*ī ūri vāru ī bhūmi krushi sesi*) and to feed 20 brahmins by its produce. This shows that the brahmins of the *agrahāra* lands had the right to sell the lands. Similar instances of the sale of the land shares in the *agrahāra* lands can also be seen in the Tamil land.[16]

The inscription discussed above mentioned that the *brahmādeya* village was organised by the *Mahājana-102* which was an organisation of landholders for village administration who exercised the right to sell the lands. The numerical suffix-102 would denote the strength of such organisation. As it had been stipulated in the grant that the land is to be cultivated by the members of the *Ur* (*ī ūri vāre krushi sesi*) which suggests the existence of cultivating tenants, who were not the members of the *mahājana* organisation. This leads to the proposition that social stratification was taking place in Andhra in the first half of 12th Century A.D.

A general survey of the land grants in the Drākshārāma temple reveals that majority of the donations were made to feed the Śiva Yōgins, brahmins ascetics and students coming from distant lands.[17] Then comes the preference of the people to provide *naivedyam*[18] for the god and then to conduct *havi, bali*, and *archana*.[19] On various occasions such as *uttarāyaṇa saṁkrānti*,[20] *Kottamāvāsya*,[21] *Gaurīvratam* and to cover the god with sandal paste[23] lands and villages were donated.

The land grants of the ladies[24] mostly belonging to the families of *mahā maṇḍalesvaras* and the royal families speak of the feminine control over the allocation of certain resources, sponsorship of specified religious rituals in the temples and earning extraordinary spiritual merit.[25] Raymond Firth made a distinction between a 'present' and 'presentation' and states that presentation is a gift conveyed in a public and formal manner with a degree of publicity.[26] The land donations of the landies to the temples or as *vṛittis* to its dependents and the epigraphical records thereof symbolize the personal qualities, common values, attitudes and relationships and publicise them as well. The gifts made by the queens of the neighbouring regions. i.e., Anantavarma Chōḍa Gaṅga's sister-in-law, the wife of Anantapāla *Daṇḍanāyaka* bespeak of the friendly ties, that they had with Chāḷukya-Chōḷas and also the role played by the women of the royal and upper class of the society in organising the state as a moral system by their *dhārmic* behaviour.

The following points can be deduced from the present study :

(1) A large number of land donations were made in the first half of 12th Century A.D. by the ministers and officials, who had the power to remit the taxes on the gifted lands.

(2) Many land transfers took place in the lower Godavari region, i.e., in the East and West Godavari district, A.P.

(3) Though the lands were purchased by paying some *māḍas,* the donors did not interfere in the enjoyment of the tillers of the soil of their respective landholdings.

(4) Communal land-holding was practised in some of the villages while individual land-holding was also practised in a lesser degree.

(5) Although it is generally held on the basis of the copper plate records of the period, that, the brahmins of the *agrahāra* lands were entitled to enjoy the land produce, privileges and had no right to sell their shares at their own will, the evidence presented above contradicts this. Further, it appears that the *mahājana* organisation had the power to sell the communal lands.

(6) The land grants made by the royal women and other ladies indicate the *dhārmic* behaviour, liberty to donate the lands, villages and to conduct certain rituals.

The concept proposed by Burton Stein[27] of the ritual sovereignty of the Chōḷa overlordship within a complex pyramidal system of political relationships" cannot be applied to the Chōḷa rule in Andhra in the first half of 12th Century A.D. as it appears from the evidence presented in the paper that Kulōttuṅga I made efforts to build up a viable, centralized administrative network to integrate the state politically. The large number of land grants made by the officials holding the titles such as *mūvendavelān, pallavarāyar* and *brahmamārāyar* as well as the land donations made by the viceroys of the period points to the Chōḻa state control that was maintained in the Āndhradēśa. Thus the present study of land grants in the Drākshārāma temple emphasizes the centralized nature of Chōḻa power and authority in the first half of 12th Century and lack of such efforts from the side of the Choḷa rulers in the succeeding periods.

NOTES AND REFERENCES

1. *S.I.I.*, Vol. IV, Nos. 1101, 1250, 1343.
2. *Ibid.*, Vol. IV, Nos. 1103, 1107, 1226, 1237, 1281, 1285, 1288, 1296, 1291.
3. N. Karashima, *South Indian History and Society—Studies from Inscriptions A.D, 850-1800*, p. xxvi.
4. *S.I.I.* Vol. IV, 1048, 1102, 1104, 1226.
5. *Ibid*. 1151,
6. *Ibid*. 1211.
7. *Ibid.*, 1343.
8. *Ibid.*, 1101.
9. *Ibid.*, 1288, 1291, 1281.
10. *Ibid.*, 1114, 1115.
11. *Ep. Ind.*, Vol. V, No. 10.
12. N. Ramesan, *Studies in Medieval Deccan, Copper Plate Inscriptions of A.P. State Museum*, pp. 115-122.
13. *Ibid.*
14. *S.I.I.*, IV, No. 1186.
15. *Ibid.*, 1281.
16. *Ibid.*, Vol. XVII, Nos. 448, 454. 460, 536 ; N. Karashima, *op. cit.* pp. 31-36.
17. *S.I.I.* Vol. IV, Nos. 1015, 1016, 1098, 1102, 1104, 1237, 1239, 1248, 1284, 1288, 1281, 1296.
18. *Ibid.*, 1101, 1133, 1152, 1182, 1186, 1203, 1291, 1371.
19. *Ibid.*, 1059, 1114, 1168, 1255, 1368.
20. *Ibid.*, 1314.
21. *Ibid.*, 1162.
22. *Ibid.*, 1043, 1373.
23. *Ibid.*, 1256, 1266.
24. *Ibid.*, 1186, 1015, 1211, 1245, 1286, 1303, 1368.
25. George W. Spencer, "When Queens bore gifts : Women as Temple Donors in the Chōḻa Period," *Śrinidhi-Perspectives in Indian Archaeology, Art and Culture*, (New Era Publications, 1983), pp. 361-373.
26. Raymond Firth, *Symbols : Public and Private* (Ithaca : Cornwell University Press, 1973), p. 376.
27. Burton Stein, *Peasant State and Society in Mediveal South India* (Oxford, 1980), p. 256.

13

IDENTIFICATION OF DUGGARAJA OF THE DRAKASHARAMA STONE INSCRIPTION

In the present paper an attempt is made to identify Duggarāja who is known in the history of the Kākatiyas by his only inscription at Drākshārāma, which is published in the South Indian Inscriptions Volume IV (No. 1071). Scholars like M. Somasekhara Sarma, P.V. Parabrahma Sastry and P. Srirama Sarma, who touched the evidence of the record were inclined to identify Duggarāja of the inscription as the son of Kākati Prōla II.[1] Though the record do not convey ano historical information as such, the proper study of it will put aside the hitherto held theory of the successful Kākatiya territorial expansion into the Coastal Andhra region in the second half of the 12th Century A.D. i.e., during the region-period of Rudradēva (A.D. 1150-1196).

The purport of the Drākshārāma inscription is to register the gift of perpetual lamp by Boppā Dēvī, wife of Duggarāja to lord Bhīmēsvara mahādēva on the occassion of vishnu saṁkrānti, in the 18th regnal year of the Chāḷukya-Chōḷa king Rājarāja and in the Śaka year 1085 (equivalent to A.D. 1163). The first two lines of the record are damaged and in the third line is mentioned Prōla as belonging to the family of Mādhavavarma to whom was born, Dugga. While referring to the gift in the last part of the record, Duggarāja is mentioned as Rēpalya Duggarāja, which was considered as the personal name by the scholars who dealt with the record earlier. But on contrary to this, it may be suggested that the term Rēpalla, which appears as a prefix to the name of Duggarāja would refer to the name of a place in Sabbināḍu of Karimnagar district. As Drākshārāma was considered as one among the five sacred Śaiva temples of the period, pilgrims from different regions used to come and worship lord Bhīmēsvara. In doing so, generally they donate lamps by giving away either 25 or 50 sheep, and the same was inscribed on the temple walls. While writing the inscriptions it was the customary practice of the temple scribes to refer to the donors alongwith their places.[2]

Nowhere in the record is stated that Prōla as the lord of Anumakoṇḍa or as belonging to the family of Kākati, like the other records of the Kākatīyas at Drākshārāma.[3] This shows that Prōla of the record under study is different from that of the Kākatīya line of rulers. In this regard, tracing the lineage to the family of Mādhavavarma needs explanation. According to two late Telugu poems, *Siddhesvara Charitramu* and *Sōmadevarājīyamu* composed in *dvipada* meter Mādhavavarma was the progenitor of the kings of Hanumakonda.[4] But curiously, none of the Kākatīya inscriptions refer to this. However, in the Anumakoṇḍa inscription dated in the year A.D. 1117, of Prōla II, his contemporary chief, Ugravādi Mēḷarasa claims to be a descendant of Mādhavavarma who possessed a great army consisting of 8000 elephants, 10 crores of horses and limitless infantry.[5] Further, in the records of the Polavāsa chiefs, whose sway extended from Polavāsa to Narasaṁpet touching Anumakoṇḍa *vishaya* in the North, Madhavavarma or Mādhava *Chakravartin* was mentioned as the founder of the family. In addition to this, on a mutilated slab in the courtyard of the temple of lord Mallesvara at Bezawāḍa also appears the *praśasti* of Madhavavarma. This undated record refers to Pallakēta Bhūpa of the Telugu Pallava family of 12th Century A.D. and mentions the boons bestowed by lord Mallesvara on Arjuna, Mādhavavarma and Paṇḍitārādhya.[6] In it, Mādhavavarma is stated to have cut-off the head of his own son, for having killed the son of a woman, selling shoots of tamarind in the Śaka year 117 (195 A.D.). On the basis of this account which also appears in the late Telugu poem, *Śrikrishṇa Vijayam* composed in A.D. 1340, which assigns Śaka 514 (A.D. 591) to Mādhavavarma, K.V. Lakshmana Rao identified him with the name-sake of the Vishṇukuṇḍin dynasty, the donor of the Pulumbūru grant and assigns him the date 594 A.D.[7] Sri M. Somasekhara Sarma who made a detailed study of the problem came to the conclusion that one Mādhavavarma flourished before Samudragupta's southern campaign who was the leader of Kshatriya immigrants into Andhra country.

Thus from the above account it is apparent that the late Telugu literary works accredit the Kakatiyas as the descendants of Mādhavavarma and as belonging to the Kshatriya caste, while the contemporary Kākatīya inscriptions are silent about this. On the other hand, their contemporary rival powers, the Polavāsa chiefs had traced their descent from Mādhavavarma in their inscriptions found at Banajipet (A.D. 1082), Medapalli (A.D. 1112), Anumakoṇḍa (A.D. 1117), and Govindapuram (A.D. 1122). Few late inscriptions of the time of Gaṇapatidēva and Rudramadēvī state that they belong to the Sūrya *vaṁśa* Kshatriya caste.[8] But the close scrutiny of other evidences reveal that they do not belong to the above said caste.[9] Therefore, it is difficult to relate this Mādhavavarma with that of the Drakshārāma record, thereby connecting Duggarāja of Rēpalla with the son of Kākati Prōla II.

Further, Dr. N. Venkataramanayya, M. Somasekhara Sarma and Dr. P. Srirama Sarma were of the opinion that the place Rēpalla was the village entrusted to Duggarāja by his brother, Rudradēva, who imposed his authority over the Gōdāvarī delta after his successful conquest of the region for a period of four or five years until A.D. 1163.[10] As the place Rēpalle in the coastal Andhra region is located near Chandolu, the capital city of the Velanāṭi Chōḷas, who were prominent at that time as the representatives of the Chāḷukya-Chōḷas in Andhra region the theory of the successful subjugation of the region by the Kākatīyas is difficult to accept. The Piṭhāpuram pillar inscription of the Haihaya chiefs[11] and an inscription at Drākshārāma[12] indicate that Prōla II was slain by a Kōṭa chief Chōdayarāja. Probably to take revenge for the death of his father, Rudra might have led his armies into the Gōdāvari region as indicated by a record at Drākshārāma dated in the 13th regnal year of the Chāḷukya-Chōḷa king, Rājarāja II and in Śaka 1080 (A.D. 1158) of Inaṁgala Brammi Reḍḍi, the *peggaḍa* of Rudradēva of Anumakonda.[13] The attempts of the Kākatīyas to conquer the coastal region were not met with success as the records of the Valanāṭi chiefs and their ministers at Drākshārāma, Chirumāmilla, Timmāpuram and other places in this period do not show any loss of territories even for a short while.[14]

It will be clear from the foregoing discussion that it is not reasonable to identify Duggarāja of Rēpalla as the son of Kākati Prōla and brother of Rudradeva, but may be considered as a ruler of Rēpalla in Sabbināḍu-1000 in the present Karimnagar district relating to the family of Polavāsa chiefs. Thus the present study shows that the Kākatīyas were not in a position to establish in the Coastal Andhra regions, and were closely followed by the powerful Polavāsa chiefs, the opposing Velanāṭi Chōḷas and the Kōṭas of Dharaṇikōṭa before they emerged as a sovereign power, i.e., in the second half of 12th Century A.D.

NOTES AND REFERENCES

1. P.V. Parabrahma Sastry, *Kākatīyas of Warangal*, p. 32, 36 ; *Telugu Samskriti*, Vol. I (Revised edition, 1983), p. 248 ; N. Venkataramanayya, and M.S. Sarma, *Early History of Deccan*, Vol. II, pp. 585, 591.
2. For example, Bhaṭṭiprōli Gōpati Seṭṭi, Bhaṭṭiprōli Kaṇchama Nāyakạ : *S.I.I.* Vol. V, No. 1154 ; 1335.

3. *Ibid.*, Nos. 1154—1335.
4. M.S. Sarma, *History of Reḍḍi Kingdoms*, 1948, p. 270.
5. *Ep. Ind.*, Vol. IX, pp. 256 ff.
6. Epigraphia Andhrica, Vol. I, p. 3 ; *I.A.P.*, Wg. No. 21 ; *I.A.P.*, Wg. No. 26.
7. M.S. Sarma, *op. cit.*, p. 268.
8. *S.I.I.*, Vol. X, No. 395, *Ep. Ind.*, Vol. XII, p. 188.
9. P.V. Parabrahma Sastry, *op. cit.*, p. 27 ; *Telugu Samskriti*, Vol. I, p. 240.
10. N. Venkataramanayya and M.S. Sarma, *op. cit.*, p. 591 ; P. Srirama Sarma, *Āndhradēśa Charitra Samskriti* (in Telugu), 1982, p. 146.
11. *Ep. Ind.*, Vol. IV ; p. 91, dated Śaka 1117 (A.D. 1195).
12. *S.I.I.*, Vol. IV, No. 1242, dated Śaka 1091 (A.D. 1169).
13. *Ibid.*, No. 1107.
14. *Ibid.*, No. 1083 ; 1086 ; 1113 ; Vol. X, No. 148, 151.

14

A RE-EXAMINATION OF THE INSCRIPTIONS OF THE KŌṬA CHIEF KĒTA II

The Kōṭa chiefs were lords of 6,000 villages on the southern bank of the river Krishṇā, conferred on them by Triṇayana Pallava. Kēta II, who was styled mahāmaṇḍalēsvara and faithful devotee of Lord Amarēsvara in his inscriptions, was the son of Kōṭa Bhīmarāja and Sabbāṁbika. So far nine inscriptions of his have been noticed and published,[1] and an attempt is made here to analyse these epigraphs critically with special reference to the symbols and figures drawn and carved on the pillars of the Amarēsvara temple at Amarāvati.

Although the date of accession of Kēta II is not mentioned in any of his records, V. Yasoda Devi agrees with Hultzsch that he came to the throne on Thursday, the 10th *tithi* of the bright fortnight of Māgha in Śaka 1104 or A.D. 1182. This date appears in seven inscriptions[2] of his, and it is supposed that the grants they record are calculated to signalize his accession.

An inscription of this kind at Amarāvati[3] dated A.D. 1182 records the grant of two lamps and the village Krantēru in the district of Kaṇḍravāḍi and the villages of Mēḍikoṇḍūru and Donkiparṛu in the district of Koṇḍa-paḍumaṭi by him and his courtesans, Gasavi Sūrama Dēvī and Prōloma Dēvī, to the Buddha. Strangely enough, the same inscription also registers the gift of villages by the same king to the Brahmins for the merit of himself, his parents and brother. Attempting to resolve this apparent paradox, Hultzsch has suggested that the two ladies who donated lamps to the Buddha may have been Buddhist *upāsikas* who induced Kēta to join them in making donations to their own god, and himself a Saivite, "to atone for his apostasy Kēta II subsequently granted a large number of villages to the Brahmins."[4]

The records of the Kōṭa chief are inscribed on the pillars at the southern entrance and eastern entrance to the central shrine of the Amarēsvara temple at Amarāvati. On the top of the grant to the Buddha, the figures of the sun, a *chauri* on either side of the standing figure of the Buddha and the crescent are carved in order from the proper right. In contradiction to these symbols, above the grant of the same chief registering donations to Siva and the Brahmins, the figures are carved of Gaṇḍabhēruṇḍa—the eagle—and seated *nandi*. Donations for the purpose of installing perpetual lamps were a common practice in the temples of the period, an instance in point being the inscription of Sōmana Peggaḍa at Drākshārāma,[5] registering the setting up of perpetual lamps at five Śaivite temples of Āndhradēśa.

It would appear that, similar pillars with the self same inscriptions once stood in the Buddhist temple which has now entirely vanished, the grants showing the catholicity of the Kōṭa chief who held the scales even among the contending religions at a time when religious disputes were rife between the Vīra-Śaivites and the Buddhists.[6]

It is passing strange that the queens of Kēta II should have associated themselves with his courtesans in making donations to temples.[7] Thus five of his wives—Vinjama Dēvī, Subbama Dēvī, Pārvatī Dēvi, Nāgama Dēvī and Komarama Dēvī and his two daughters—Sabbamma Dēvī and Lakshmī Dēvī, jointly made donations of lamps with six of his concubines—Kasadi Sūrama Dēvī, Bhaṇḍāruvu Prōlama Dēvī, Bhaṇḍāruvu Nāgima Dēvī, Chōḍama Dēvī, Guṇḍama Dēvī and Gadya Vīrama Dēvī—to Śiva at Amarāvati, while Kasadi Sūrama Dēvī, Arama, Kētama and Guṇḍā Dēvī made gifts to Rāmēsvara at Vēlpūru.[8] There is no evidence that these courtesans of Kēta were Buddhist *upāsikas*, as suggested by Hultzsch. Rather they were tolerant towards Buddhism although Śaivites themselves, as their donations to Śiva are more in number than to the Buddha. It is also clear from the inscriptions that though polygamy was in practice, the chiefs had many women as their courtesans. The latter enjoyed high social status and moved freely with the *Kulastrīs* of the royal household. Raymond Firth has truly remarked that "gifts are often judged not primarily as a contribution to resources, but as an index to the attitude of the giver."[9] The donations made by the ladies of Kēta II as a well-publicised form of symbolic expression conveys the impression that they were the upholders of social and religious values through the generous support to temples and Brahmins.

While studying the records of Kēta II, it has been observed that a record[10] of his in Sanskrit and Telugu registering the gifts of certain villages which were named after his father, mother and brother to Brahmins was inscribed at two places, Amarāvati and Vēlpūru. In both of them, the content and date of the grants are identical. Further, the same kind of information is repeated in some of his records.[11] More significant is the information given in a record from Amarāvati dated 1197 A.D.[12] that when the seven *agrahāra* villages viz. Guntūru, Polasilmirṟu, Kocchera, Vaṁggīpuram, Inugallu, Upputūru and Kāremchēḍu originally granted by Mukkanti Kāḍuveṭti were disturbed, Kēta II had them restored to the Brahmins. The first part of the above-said information is confirmed by the Koṇidena inscription of Annamantri,[13] which states that Rudrabhaṭṭa, the progenitor of the family, had received Vaṁggīpura *agrahara* from Triṇayana Pallava. This inscription is undated, but palaeographically it belongs to the 12 Century A.D. Further the issuer of the record Annamantri, was the minister of Nanni Chōḍa, the Telugu Chōḷa ruler who ruled from 1151-1160 A.D. Whether Trilōchana Pallava or Mukkanṭi Kāduveṭti was historical or not, some Pallava ruler who had effective rule over the present Guntur district sometime before the advent of the Eastern Chāḷukyas, may have granted the village to him. The village granted can be identified with Vangīpuram in Bapatla Taluq of Guntur district. As this record is silent about the distress caused in *agrahāra* villages this event can be placed after A.D. 1160 and before A.D. 1197, the date of Kēta II's record.

For the reasons of the distress caused in the seven *agrahāra* villages, the inscriptions provide no clues. It could have been due to the civil war in Palnad, the story of which is chronicled in the Telugu poem, *Palnātivīra Charita*. The battle of Kāreṁpūḍi took place in the middle of A.D. 1184,[14] and probably as a result of it the *agrahāra* villages might have been disturbed.

In the Mogaluṭla copper plate grant of Gaṇapāṁba[15] of Śaka 1141 (A.D. 1219), Kēta II has been referred to as the donor of seven villages (*grāma saptati dānāṁbu saritpūrita sāgaraḥ*). In this context, it should be noted here that, although Kēta II made the donation of twenty-five villages, he is especially remembered for the re-establishment of the seven *agrahāra* villages which were once given by Triṇayana Pallava to the Brahmins. It was the sacred study of the ruler to protect and to safeguard the duration of the donations made, and as this had been done by Kēta II, he was well remembered in the time of Gaṇapama Dēvī, as the donor of the seven villages, though thirty-seven years had passed since their restoration.[16]

It will follow from the above that in this period Buddha was worshipped in human form as a god in the temple by setting up lamp donations. The liberal donations made by the courtesans of Kēta II along with his family members reveal the important part played by the women of the royal household in allocating resources to temples and Brahmins, thus enhancing the royal prestige. The identical records of Kēta II at Amarāvati and

Vēlpūru stating his donation of villages to Brahmins can only be viewed in the process of publicising the gifts made by him as soon as he came to the throne.

NOTES AND REFERENCES

1. *Ep. Ind.*, Vol. VI, No. 15-A, pp. 146-157 ; *A.R.* 262 of 1897 ; S.I.I., Vol. III, Nos. 224, 228, 229, 236 ; *Ibid.*, Vol. X, pp. 198-200.
2. *Ep. Ind.*, Vol. VI, No. 15-A, *S.I.I.*, Vol. VI, Nos. 224, 236, *Ibid.*, Vol. X, Nos. 198, 199, 200 ; *A.R.* No. 262 of 1897.
3. *Ep. Ind.*, Vol. VI, No. 15-A, pp. 146-157.
4. *Ibid.*, p. 148.
5. *S.I.I.*, Vol. IV, No. 749.
6. Krishna Kumari, M., *The Rule of the Chalukya-Cholas in Andhradesa*, (Delhi, 1985), pp. 215-217.
7. *S.I.I.*, Vol. VI, No. 228.
8. *Ibid.*, Vol. X, Nos. 249, 252, 260.
9. Raymond Firth, *Symbols : Public and Private* (Ithaca : Cornwell University Press, 1973), p. 372.
10. *S.I.I.*, Vol. VI, No. 236, *Ibid.*, Vol. X, No. 199.
11. *Ep. Ind.*, Vol. VI, No. 15, pp. 148-153.
12. *S.I.I.*, Vol. VI, No. 228.
13. *Ibid.*, No. 620 ; C. Somasundara Rao, "Konidena Inscription of Anna-mantri," *Svasti Śrī*, Dr. B. Ch. Chabbra Felicitation Volume, Delhi, 1984, 14, pp. 113-115.
14. *Epigraphia Andhrica*, Vol. IV, 1975, pp. 93-102.
15. *S.I.I.*, Vol. VI, Nos. 229, 236, *Ibid.*, Vol. X, No. 198.
16. B.V. Krishna Rao, *History of the Eastern Chāḷukyas of Vēngi (A.D. 610-1210)*, Hyderabad, 1973, p. 577.

15

YUDDHAPURA PLATES OF RAJARĀJA DĒVĒNDRA, VARMA, Ś 998

This copper plate along with the copper plate grant of king Rājēndravarman was discovered in the month of May, 1985 while digging for the bricks in the fields near to the temple of Kāmaliṅgēsvarasvāmi at Gallavalli. Gallavalli is a small village and is about 15 km. away from Rajam in Bobbili Taluk of Vizianagaram District, Andhra Pradesh.

The inscription is written on three plates, each measuring 25.5 cms. by 12.5 cms. The thickness of the plates is 6 cms. and the ring-hole diameter is 2 cms. These plates were stung together on a ring, and the ends of it were soldered below the king's seal. The seal of the plates contains a seated *nandi* in relief, like the one on the top of a pillar and is associated with the usual Eastern Gāṅga emblems of sun, moon, *ankuśa,* sword to the right and drum, conch and *chāmara* to the left. The weight of the plates with the ring and the seal is 3.700 gms. The third plate is inscribed only on the inner side while the other two plates bave inscription on both the sides. There are altogether 47 lines of writing. Their distribution on the various faces of the plates being as follows : IIIA—9 lines, IIA—10 lines, IIB—10 lines, IA—10 lines, IB—8 lines. The edges of the plates are raised into rims and the preservation of the inscription is satisfactory. An interesting fact about the record is that the beginning of the document is written on the inner side of the third plate, continued on both the sides of the second plate followed by the inner side and finally completed on the outer side of the first plate. Moreover, the inscription is incomplete and ended abruptly without any usual imprecatory or benedictory verses and of any reference to the officials or scribes who were responsible for the preparation of the document. Two other records of the king, issued in the same year also ends abruptly in the same manner.[1]

The script of the inscription is Kaliṅga Nāgari of 11th Century A.D. It is the same as that employed in the copper plate grants of the early members of the Imperial Gāṅga family.[2] The language used in the record is Sanskrit and is composed in both prose and verse. The *praśasti* of the Eastern Gāṅga family and the genealogy mentioned in the present grant are identical with the other grants of the same king. As regards the orthography also, the inscription closely resembles the other copper plate records of the king. Like the records of Vajrahasta III the sign for v is used for b also, as in *mahāśavda* for *mahāśabda* (1.6), *samupalavdha* for *samupalabdha* (1.7), *śākāvde* for *śākābde* (1.25, 38, 46). Incorrect spellings such as *siṅgha* for *siṁha* (1.38), *subhe* for *śubhe* and *saṁśikta* for *saṁsikta* (1.39). Final forms of the letters are expressed by giving a stroke below the letter, as in *nivahān* (1.11) and *vāraṇān* (1.31).

The date of the charter is given in the chronogram *vasu-nanda-nidhi* of the Śaka era, i.e., Śaka 998, while the details of the date quoted are *vishuvu-saṁkrānti* in the month of *Tulā*. The date of the grant thus appears to be 1076 A.D.

The purport of the inscription is to record the gift of the village Yuddhapura in Saṁvā-*vishaya* by Rājarāja Dēvēndravarma to Pallaya Śa(rma), son of Durggaya Śarma, for the increase of the merit and fame of the king and his parents.

King Rājarāja Dēvēndravarma issued the grant from Kaliṅganagara, which can be identified with Mukhalingam in the Srikakulam district. He was styled as *Parama-māhēsvara* and *Parama-bhaṭṭāraka* and *Trikaliṅgādhipati*.

In the *praśasti*, the Gāṅgas are described as the rulers of Tri-Kaliṅga and as belonging to the Ātreya *gōtra*, and as having obtained the conch-shell, drum, the five great sounds, the white umbrella, the golden fly-whisk and the bull-emblem or crest by the grace of lord Gōkarṇasvāmi (1.5, 6).

The following is the genealogy mentioned in the present grant (9-35), which agrees with that referred to in the other copper plate records of Vajrahasta III, the father and predecessor of the issuer of the present grant as well as the records of Anantavarma Chōḍa Gaṅga,[3] his son and successor.

Guṇamahārṇava

|

Vajrahasta (I) 44 years

|

Guṇḍama (I) 3 years	Kāmārṇava (I) 35 years Vajrahasta (II) alias Aniyaṅka Bhīma 35 years	Vinayāditya 3 years

Kāmārṇava (II) ½ year married Vinaya Mahādēvī of Vaidumba family	Guṇḍama (II) 3 years	Madhu Kāmārṇava 19 years

|

Anantavarma Vajrahasta (III)
(coronation in Ś 960)
33 years, married Anaṅga
Mahādēvī

|

Rājarāja Dēvēndravarma
(coronation in Śaka 992)
donor of the present grant.

While making the donation, like the other village grants of Rājarāja Dēvēndravarma,[4] the present charter also do not refer to it as an *agrahāra* donation. Thereby it appears that the donee Pallaya (Śarma) is liable to pay rent or cess for his holdings.

As regards the gift-village, Yuddhapura, it may be identified with the present day Vuddavolu in Bobbili Taluk of Vizianagaram District.[5] It is stated in the record that the gift village is located in Saṁvā *vishaya.* The same district is known from the records of Vajrahasta III,[6] Anantavarma Chōḍa Gaṅga Dēva[7] and Rājarāja Dēvēndravarma[8] and is considered that it would correspond to present day Chipurupalle and Bobbili Taluks of Vizianagaram District. The donee is mentioned in the grant as the resident of the village Śrīpura. The village is mentioned in Kōrōshanda grant of Viśākhavarman, the ruler of Kaliṅga.[9] It may be identical with Siripuram in Visakhapatnam district, three miles south of the Nāgāvaḷi river.[10]

TEXT[11]

(Metres : 1, 3, 11, 13, 16—*Śārdūlavikrīḍita* ; 2, 6, 12, 14—*anushṭubh* ; 4—*Vaṁśastha* ; 5, 9—*Mālinī* ; 7, 8 Gīti ; *Third Plate* : *First side* : 10, 15 *Vasanta tilaka*) 7, 8 *Gīti* ;

1. Ōṁ[12] Svasti Śrīmatām=akhila—bhuvana-vinuta-nayavinaya-dayā-dāna-dākshiṇya/[13] satya-
2. śaucha-śauyya-dhairyya-ādi-guṇa-ratna-pavitrakāṇaṁ-Ātrēya-gotrā-ṇāṁ-vimala-vichā(r)-
3. āchāra-puṇya-salila-prakshyālita—Kāli-kāla-kalmasha-mashīṇāṁ mahā-Mahendr-āchala-śi-
4. khara-pratishṭitasya sa-char-āchara gurōḥ sakala-bhuvana-nirmāṇ-aika-sūtradhāra-
5. sya śaśāṅka—chūḍāmaṇer=bbhagavatō Gōkarṇṇasvāminaḥ prasā-dāt=samāsādit –ai-
6. ka śaṅkha-bhērī-pañcha-mahāśavda(bda)-dhavala—chchatra-hēma-chāmara-vara-vṛishabha-lāñchhana-
7. samujvala-samasta-sāmrājya-mahīm-anēka-samara-saṅghaṭṭa-samu-palavdha(bdha)-Vijayalakshmī-(samā)-
8. liṅgit-ōttuṅga-bhuja-daṇḍa-maṇḍitā nāṁ Trikaliṅga-mahībhujāṁ Gaṅganāṁ=anvayam=alaṅka (rishṇōr).
9. Vvishṇor=iva Vikram—ākrānta-dharā-maṇḍa lasya Guṇa mahā (rṇa) va-mahārājasya (pu)

II Plate : *First side* :

10. //(traḥ)//o//[14] Pūrva bhūpatibhir=vvibhajya vasudhāya pañchatiḥ pañchadhā-bhuktā-bhūri-parākramō=bhu-
11. ja balāt=tam=ēkagra=svayaṁ (yaṁ)-ekī kṛitya=vijitya śattru-nivahān śrī-Vajra hastas'=chatus'=chatvarimśa.
12. tam=atyudāra—charitaḥ sarvām=arakshīt=samāḥ//(1) Tasya tanayō Guṇḍama—rājā (jō) varsha-trayam=apālaya-
13. d-bbahīṁ//Tad-anujaḥ Kāmārṇavadēvāḥ pañcha-triṁśatam=avda (abda) kān/Tasy-ānujō=Vinayādityas=samā-
14. s=tisraḥ/Tataḥ Kāmārṇṇavaj=jāto jagatā—kalpabhūruhaḥ/Yō-rājad=rājita—chchhāyō Vajrahastō-

15. Vanī patiḥ/(2) Prasthodan-mada-gandha-luvdha (bdha)-madhupa-vyālīḍha-gadhān=gajann=artthi bhyas=samadā-
16. t=sahasram=atulō yas=tyāginām=agraṇīssaḥ śrīmān=Aniyaṅka Bhīma nṛipatir=Gang-ānvay-ōttaṁ-
17. sakaḥ pañcha-triṁśatam=avda (bda) kān=sama bhunak=prith-vīṁ stutaḥ pārtthivaiḥ//(3) Tad-agra-sūnuḥ-surarāja-
18. sūnuna samas=samastāṁ samit-arimaṇḍalah(/) Sma pāti Kāmārṇ-ṇava-bhūpatir=bbhuvam samṛiddhimān-
19. arddha-samāṁ samujvalaḥ//(4) Tad-anu tad-anu-janmā chittajanm-ōpamānō guṇa nidhir=anavadyō.

II Plate : *Second side* :

20. Guṇḍam—ākhyō mahīśaḥ (/) sakalam—idam=arakshatt-rīṇi-varshāṇi dhātrī-valayam=alaghu-tejō-nirjji-
21. t-arati chakraḥ//(5) Tatō dvaimātura=tasya Madhukāmārṇṇavo nṛipah / Avati—smāvanīm=ētām=avdā(abda)m-
22. ekānna—viṁśatiṁ//(6) Atha vajrahasta-nṛipater—agra-sutād=akhila-guni-Janāgra (ga) ṇyaḥ (/) Kāmā-
23. ravān 1 kav-īndra-pragīyamān-āvada ta śubha kīrttiḥ//(7) Śriya iva vaidumb-anvaya-payaḥ-payō-
24. nidhi-samdbhavāyāś=chayaḥ samajani vinaya mahādēvyāḥ Śrī Vajrahasta=iti ta-
25. nayaḥ//(8) *viyad-ri* (*ṛi*) *tu-nidhi-saṁ khyāṁ yāti śak-āv*(*b*)*da saṁkh*(*y*) *ē dinā kṛi ti vṛi shabhaste* (*sthe*) Rō . (hi)-
26. *nī bhē su lagne* (/) *Dhanushi ca sita-pakshe sūryya vāre tritiyā* yuji sakala dharitriṁ rakshi (tuṁ)-
27. yō=bhishiktaḥ//(9) Nyāyāyyēṇa yatra samam=ācharituṁ tri-vargge=(rggaṁ) mārggeṇa rakshati mahīm-mahita pratāpē (/)-
28. Nirvvyadhayaś=cha nirghāś=cha nirāpadaś=cha śaśvat=prajā bhuvi bhavanti (ntu) vibhūti-matyāḥ//(10) Vyāpte . (Ga)-
29. ṅga-kul-ōttamasya yaśasa dik-chakravāle śaśi-pra . . (dyōt)-āmali nena yasya bhuvanaḥ . . (prahlā)-

I Plate : *Second side* :

30. da-sampādinām (/) Saindūre-ati-sāndra-paṅka patalaiaḥ kunta sthali paṭṭakesvālimpanti punaḥ pu

31. naś=cha haritām=ādhoraṇā vāranān (/) (/) (11) Anurāgeṇa guṇino yasya vaksho mukh-āvj(bj) ayōḥ/.

32. Āsīnē Śrī Sarasvatyāv=anukūlē virājataḥ[15]//o//Āgachchannuru vikrameṇa—sahasā—śāstr=ā bhi.

33. dhātat—vibhoy—ēkā—vyāhata-visvavṛtti—mahimā—helā—nirastō—ganiḥ / Ten—ākāri—nikāma—kāmya-

34. tanunā-rājyaṁ-mahī-maṇḍale-triṁ śad-vatsara-mabhra-subhra-yaśasā·varshatrayēṇādhikaṁ//(13)[16] Tatō-

35. naṅga-mahādēvyām Vajrahasta-mahī patēh / Gauryāmiva-Harasy=ābhūt=Kārttike ya-iv-

36. ātmajaḥ ‖ (14) lakshmī-vadhū-vadana-paṅkajam—ākaranda-sandōha-chāru-pari-chumva(mba)na-chaṁcharīka-

37. ḥ/yo māninām-cha-guṇinām—cha-duratmanāṁ-cha-sāntiṁ-cha-mōdama-tulaṁ-cha-bhayaṁ-cha-datte ‖ (15) *Śā-*

38. *kāvdɛ(bdɛ) nayanāvja (bja)-garbha nidhiśe jeṣṭeṣṭamī-siṅgha(ṁhi) ke-lagne-chottara-phālguṇiśu-guru-dine-pakshe-*

39. *su—subhre*—subhe—lokālōka—mahā—mahā-dhavalāyalaṁkāra—vatyā-bhuva—saṁ-sikta-ssa-ka.

I Plate : First side :

40. lingarāja-tilakaḥ-Śrī-Rājarājonṛpah //o// (16)[17] Kaliṅganagarān-parama-mahēsvara-parama-

41. bhaṭṭāraka-mahārājādhirāja—*trikaliṅgādhipati*—Śrī-mad-*Dɛvɛndra-varmā—Rājarāja de-*

42. vaḥ—kuśalī—samast=āmātya-pramukha-janapadān—samāhūya-samājñāpayati—vidi-

43. tam=astu—bhavataṁ / *Saṁvā Vishayɛ Yuddha purākhyō—grāmaś—*chaturs—sīm-ā-

44. vachchinnas-sajala stalas-sarvva-pīḍā-vivarjjitām—āchandr-ārkka-kshiti sama-kālaṁ-

45. yāvan-mātā-pitrōr-ātmanaś-cha puṇya-yaśo-bhi-vṛiddhaye-*vasu-nanda-nidhi-ga-*

46. *ṇite-śākā vde(bde)*[18] *Tulā-māse-vishuvati-samkrān-tyāṁ / Śrīpura-grāma-nivāsi* /[19] . (śa)-

47. ṇḍilya-gōtra-vājasanēyaka / Durgga ya-Śarmmanaḥ putrāya Pallaya-śa . . (rmmaṇaḥ ?)

NOTES AND REFERENCES

1. *J.A.H.R.S.*, Vol. XXVIII, pp. 238 ff ; *Ibid.*, Vol. XX, pp. 171-176 ; *Ep. Ind.*, Vol. XXXI, No. 24, pp. 191-196.
2. For a list of inscriptions, of Vajrahasta III, father of Rājarāja Dēvēndravarma, who issued the copper plates under study, See *Ep. Ind. Vol.* XXXII, p. 310 f. n. 3 ; N. Ramesan, *Copper Plate Inscriptions of Andhra Pradesh Government Museum*, Vol. I, p. 137 ff ; C. Somasundara Rao, *Epigraphia Andhrica*, Vol. IV, pp. 25-34 ; See also, Rājarāja Dēvēndra Varma's own grants (Ch. No. 4 of 1918-19), *J.A.H.R.S.*, Vol. VIII, pp. 171 ff, also *Ibid.*, Vol. XX, pp. 171-176, and the same published in *Ep. Ind.*, Vol. XXXI, No. 24, pp. 191-196.
3. Excepting the Vizāgapaṭam plates of Anantavarma Chōḍa Gaṅga, dated Śaka 1040 (*I.A.*, XVIII, pp. 165 ff.), his Korni plates, dated Śaka 1034 (*J.A.H.R.S.*, Vol. I, pp. 106 ff.) and Chinna Badamu plates, dated in Śaka 1062 (*Epigraphia Andhrica*, Vol., II, pp. 56-72). These plates state that Vajrahasta was the son of Madhukāmarṇava.
4. *Ep. Ind.*, Vol. XXXI, No. 24, pp. 191-196 ; *J.A.H.R.S.*, Vol. VIII, pp. 176 ff.
5. It has been observed that the place names ending with *pura* and *puram* had been substituted by *Prōlu* or *ōlu*, in course of time. For example, Krishṇarāya *puram* had been changed to Koppōlu (Cuddapah Dist.) and Niravadya *pura* to Nidada *vōlu* (E. "Godavari Dist.) ; P. Nagamalleswara Rao, "Renaming in Telugu Place Names," *Studies in Indian Place Names*, Vol. VI, pp. 71-86.
6. V. Ramesan, *Copper Plate Inscriptions of Andhra Pradesh Government Museum*, Vol. I, p. 144.
7. *Ibid.*, pp. 154-55 ; I.A., XVIII, pp. 161 ff ; and p. 165 ff.
8. N. Ramesan, *op. cit.*, pp. 154-55.
9. *Ep. Ind.*, Vol. XXI, p. 24.
10. The Bhūmikhaṇḍa of the *Padmapurāṇa* mentions the city as situated in Kaliṅga.
11. From the Plates and the impressions.
12. Expressed by symbol.
13. The punctuation mark is necessary.
14. The punctuation mark indicates the separation of the following part in verse from the foregoing section in prose.
15. There are two double *daṇḍas* here, with a globular mark between them, to indicate the separation of the foregoing part quoted from the grants of Vajrahasta III from the following portion composed by the court poet of Rājarāja.
16. To the description of Vajrahasta III, this stanza was added by the court poet of Rājarāja I.
17. There are two double *daṇḍas* here, with a globular mark between them, to indicate the separation of the foregoing introductory part in verse from the following grant portion in prose.
18. The punctuation mark is unnecessary.
19. This is to indicate that the donee was a resident of the village Śrīpura.

SECTION—II

1

LAKSHMĪNĀRĀYANASVĀMY TEMPLE AT AVANIGADDA

Avanigadda is situated on the left bank of the river Krishṇā. It is a small village in Divi Taluk in Krishna District of Andhra Pradesh. There are four inscriptions in the temple, the texts of which are all published in *South Indian Inscriptions*, Volume IV.[1] At present only two records are to be seen in the temple, one inscribed on a pillar and the other on a slab which was placed in front of the door of the *antarāla* of the temple. Of the records published, the earliest[2] is dated in Śaka 1060, corresponding to A.D. 1138 and the latest record[3] is dated in Ś 1076 (=A.D. 1154). Locally, the temple is known as Lakshmīnārāyaṇasvāmy temple. But it is of interest to note that in the records of the temple the God to whom the gifts were made is mentioned as Chōḍanārāyaṇa and the place is referred to as Dhanadavrōlu. Dr. V. Yasodadevi mentioned that the temple of Dhanadavrōlu Chōḍa Nārāyaṇadēva was at Avanigadda.[4] But it is clear from the study of the records of the period that Dhanadavrōlu refers to the name of a place and Chōḍa Nārāyaṇa to lord Viṣṇu, who is named after Chōḍa. In the present paper it is aimed to study in detail the inscriptions and the architectural details of the temple.

As stated earlier, the records are four in number and are inscribed by Kāpāchāri. The language of the records in Telugu verse and prose. It is of interest to note that these few records of the temple register the gifts made by certain ladies for their own merit and do not belong to any king or chief ruling over that area. These records are the lamp grants, dated in Śaka years and do not refer to the regnal years of the reigning Chāḷukya-Chōḷa kings. It appears from the records under study that Chintamanāyaka was a favourite and faithful servant of Velanāṭi Gonka (II) and the lord of Kollūru. His son was Muttama Nāyaka, to whom were born two daughters—Kommama and Nūṁkama. Muttama Nāyaka was mentioned as *Paḍihāri* of Velanāṭi chief Gonka II (1136-1162/63 A.D.). From the inscriptions it is evident that, to provide 1 *māna* of ghee daily for the upkeep of a perpetual lamp, it requires 16 *birudgadyas* or 55 sheep.

As far as we know, the place Dhanadavrōlu refers to the capital city of the Velanāṭi chiefs which is variously mentioned as Sanadavrōlu,[5] Dhanadavrōlu[6] and Dhanadapura[7] in the records of Drākshārāma, Chandolu, Timmāpuram and Pithapuram. Mañchana in his work, *Kēyūrabāhucharitra* mentioned the name of the place as Dhanadapuram and describes it, as being enriched with the fields of sugarcane gardens, several tanks and temples.[8] It is identified with the present-day village, Chandolu in Bapatla Taluk of Guntur District. The Viṣṇu temple at Chandolu is known as Chennakēśava temple and is barren of records. Though the name Avanigadda is not noticed in any of the inscriptions of the period, it is reasonable to suggest that Dhanadavrōlu, at which the temple of Chōḍa Nārāyaṇa is located, is the same as the present-day Avanigadda. As to the name of the temple, it could have been so named after the Velanāṭi Chief Rājēndra Chōḍa I (A.D. 1109-1136-37), the son of Velanāṭi Gonka I.

The temple of Lakshmīnārāyaṇasvāmy is an interesting structure as it preserves in it an admixture of different conventions and reveals the character of later Chōḷa, later Chāḷukyan and Hoysala temple architecture. The temple is situated within a rectangular brick-built enclosure at the centre of the village with an entrance towards East (Pl. 1). This entrance has a lofty *gōpura*, which is a tall and narrow structure. The base and the wall-portion is built of stone and the superstructure is made of bricks consisting of six storeys. The base of the *gōpura* contains from bottom to top *upāna, jagati, Tripaṭṭa Kumuda, Kanṭha* and *Paṭṭika* (Pl. 2). The Eastern *gōpura* has a *manḍapa* consisting of two compartments on either side of the entrance. Each section of the *manḍapa* has one pillar simply carved. The doorway of the *gōpura* flanked by Vaiṣṇava *dvārapālakas* shows good work. Above the *dvārapālakas* is carved the elaborate floral design carried upto the top. At the centre of the top of the doorway is carved the figure of Gajalakshmī. On the outer wall surface of the *gōpura* facing the main street of the village are carved the two symbols of Vaiṣṇavite faith, *Śaṅkha* and *Chakra* on the right and left side of the entrance. The outer walls of the *gōpura* towards the North and South are carefully modelled. The wall space is used to accommodate the niches or *dēvakōṣhṭhas* (Pl. 3). The pilasters are present and their slender shafts divide the wall portion into five rectangular compartments in the shape of miniature shrines. Of them, the middle niche is wider than the other four which are of equal proportions. This division of the wall into well proportioned areas gives it a functional frame work of great architectural value. Above the two closely flanking pilasters of the niche, is carved the replica of *dravidian śikhara* (Pl. 2). Some of the later Chāḷukyan temples found in the Telangana region of Andhra Pradesh, for example Chennakēsava temple at Gangapur and Pachchala Sōmēsvara temple at Pānugal also contain *dravidian* spire motif on the projections of the exterior walls of the *garbha-gṛiha* and *antarāla*.[9] Moreover, in the temples of Karnataka, this convention of decorating the exterior walls with the *Dravida vimāna* models is found besides other temples on the walls of Kālidēva temple at Bagli, Tārakēsvara temple at Hangal, Siddhēsvara temple at Haveri, Mallēsvara temple at Kikkēri, Tripurāntakēsvara temple at Balagamre, Chennakēsava temple at Marale.[10] Over the *sikhara* portion of the *dēvakoṣṭa* is carved the *Vyāla* with protruding eyes, horns, wide-opened mouth and 4 legs in a seated posture. Just below the top of all the pilasters is carved the heads of the serpents. The images in the niches are carved in relief. They include seated Gaṇeśa, three-hooded serpent, *Kāli*, *Ādimūrti* with his consort Lakshmī and five-hooded serpent above, Viṣṇu seated, Narasiṁha with his consort, Krishṇa, *Pañchānana* Śiva (Pl. 8) and the figure of a lady seated with an attendant facing a male in lying posture on a bed. Above the images an architrave is carved with or without the lion's head on the top. The details of the sculptures show the Chōḷa craftsmanship. The niches are similar to the types seen in the temples of Biccavolu. But the *makaratōraṇa* on top of the *dēvakōṣṭas*, the chief architectural motif in the Chāḷukya temples in Andhra is absent in the temple under study. On top of the niches are arranged friezes in narrow horizontal bands including the floral designs and over it, is a band of swans in frontal exposition. Beautifully carved pillars at Pattadakal and carvings on a huge block at Kailāsanātha temple, Ellora, paved the way towards medieval frieze depictions. The Hoysalas brought the friezes to its final perfected form.[11] The *adhiṣṭāna* of the Sangamēsvara temple at Kudavalli (Alampur Taluk) is embellished with a variety of sculptures unlike the other Chāḷukyan temples.[12] In the temple under study the frieze components are already fully defined and might have had the influence from the Hoysala frieze sculptures.

The proper temple is situated in the centre of a rectangular courtyard. It is constructed on a high podium of *upapīṭha* (Pls. 4, 5, 6). *Upapīṭha* is generally placed below the *adhistana*. In the early Chōḷa temples it is simple in design and is represented as a sort of giant *kanṭha* with tall supporting rectangular planks.[13] The Chāḷukyan temples at Aihole, Badami, Pattadakal, Alampur, Biccavolu, Drākshārāma and Pondugula are devoid of *upapīṭha*. Similarly, the Pallava, Rāsṭrakūta and Pāṇḍya temples are also not provided with *upapīṭha*.[14] According to S.R. Balasubramanyam, the early Chōḷa temples do not contain *upapīṭha*.[15] But in the temples constructed by the later Chōḷas, the later Chaḷukyas and Hoysalas of Dvārasamudra, the *upapīṭha* occupied a position of great importance. *Upapīṭha* is not exactly rectangular in shape, but its sides project or recede being carried parallel to the lines and angles of the building it supports. The platform is quite spacious and thus provides a suitable substitute for procession or circumambulation. The Hoysalesvara temple at Halebid, Somesvara temple at Gadag, the Mahādēva temple at Ittagi and Mahādēva temple at Sinnar show that the *upapīṭha* is projected beyond the shrine proper thus leaving a broad flat surface around the temple for outer *pradakshiṇāpatha*.[16]

The *upapītha* rests on *upāna*, which is straight in profile and projecting beyond *jagati*. *Jagati* is vertical and in line with the top of *upapītha*. Above it, is *paṭṭika*, the most significant and common architectural element in *upapīṭha*. Between the *paṭṭikas* is used *padma* moulding in two forms—*mahāpadma* and *alpapadma*. Another important element is *tripaṭṭa kumuda*. It is hewn horizontally into one vertical and two raking faces. Above and below *tripaṭṭa kumuda* is the recessed moulding known as *kanṭha* or neck. It has a vertical surface and is used to connect *mahāpadma* and *alpapadmas* with *tripaṭṭakumuda*. The *upapīṭha* is devoid of figure sculpture except two animal carvings found on the projections towards the South-West corner of the temple. Two stylised lions and two elephants are carefully carved below *tripaṭṭakumuda* (Pls. 5 and 6).

The temple is approached by a flight of steps from the East, the North and the South, which are flanked by *ratha* type mouldings. The *mukhamaṇḍapa* of the temple is a rectangular pillared hall with 14 pillars (Pl. 7). Of them, the front two pillars are of *Vyāla* type. The shaft of the pillar is carved with the figure of a seated lion. Above it, is the rounded pillar with the neck-moulding (*padma-bandha*). On top of it, is a great lotus (*padma*), wide open in lovely *cyma recta*, the tips of petals curving inwards to make strong torus moulding. On *padma* rests a wide square block, the *phalaka* or abacus. Percy Brown observed that the expansion of *phalagai* or plank is the most striking element in the Chōḷa pillar and capital.[17]

The other type of pillars used in the *mukhamaṇḍapa* are of *citrakhaṇḍa* type. They are with square base, an octagonal shaft, a short *lāśuna*, a heavy ribbed *ghaṭa* and a *pōtika*. The shaft is cut into 16 sides with an interesting octagonal band. There are eight such pillars in the mandapa. Another type of pillars in the *mukhamaṇḍapa* shows square base and square shaft. Separating the shaft and capital is a narrow recessed moulding, *padma-bandha*. Above it, is *padma* and *phalaka*. The ceiling of *mukhamaṇḍapa* is lozenge shaped. The *mukhamaṇḍapa* leads to the closed *antarāḷa*. The doorway of *antarāḷa* is flanked by Vaiṣṇava *dvārapālakas*. Above it, is carved the floral designs and on top of the doorway is carved the figure of Gajalakshmī. On the exterior walls of the *gōpura, brahmakānta* type of pillars and pilasters are used with the figures of *Nāgas* on the abacus. The ceiling of the *antarāḷa* is lozenge shaped. An inscribed slab is placed in front of the entrance of *antarāḷa*.

The *garbha-gṛiha* is square in plan. The door jamb is carved with *pūrṇakuṁbhas* and floral designs. Gajalakshmī is carefully carved on top of the entrance. The ceiling of the sanctum sanctorum is lozenge shaped. The icon of the temple is Lakshmīnārāyaṇasvāmy with serpent hood above. To the right side of the sanctum, is appended a small shrine facing east. The *adhiṣṭāna* of the temple consists of *Upāna, tripaṭṭakumuda, Kanṭha* and two *Mahāpadmas* (Pl. 5). At the rear of the sanctum, i.e., towards west is a *Koṣṭapañjara*, a simple rectangular recess with two pilasters without any image. The small shrine to the right side of the sanctum is devoid of *adhiṣṭāna* mouldings and is with 4 *Siṁhapāda* pillars towards the south and north. Joining these pillars brick-walls are constructed. Definitely this could have been an addition made in the later times. Above the wall portion of the sanctum is a row of swans. The *śikhara* of the temple is renovated and built of bricks. The *Vimāna* contains the series of *pañjara, kūṭa, sāla* and *pañjara* decorations with four seated lions in the four corners. There are 12 *siṁhalalāṭa* gables with deity sculptures.

Thus a careful study of the architectural features of the Viṣṇu temple at Avanigadda and the inscriptional evidence of the place leads to the following conclusions :

(1) The temple is constructed in the 1st quarter of 12th Century A.D. and is named after the Velanāṭi chief, Rājēndra Chōḍa I as Chōḍa Nārāyaṇa temple.

(2) On the circumstantial evidence, the place Dhanadavrōlu may be identified with Avanigadda.

(3) The construction of the temple on a raised platform called *upapīṭha* is a new architectural element and is not present in the early Chāḷukyan temples of Āndhradēśa. The Chōḷa temples from the time Rājarāja I in Tamilnadu the later Chālukyan temples and the temples of Hoysalas in Karnataka, the Kākatīya temples in Telangana present this characteristic architectural element.

(4) Unlike the *upapīṭhas* of the Hoysala temples, which are lavishly decorated with floral, geometrical, animal and figural motifs, the

temple under study is devoid of figure-sculpture, except two animal reliefs on the South-West corner.

(5) Unlike some of the early Chāḷukyan temples the temple at Avanigadda is a *nirandhara* shrine and the *pradakshiṇa* is to be made around the temple on the broad space left on top of the *upapīṭhas*. Similarly, in most of the later Chāḷukyan and Hoysala temples, the inner *pradakshiṇāpatha* is absent.

(6) The outer-walls of the Eastern *gōpura* are decorated with structural motifs and sculptures. *Dēvakoṣṭas* or niches are formed by two slender pilasters surmounted by *draviḍa vimāna* in between the pilasters. The Karnataka models are more ornamented and canopied by *makaratoraṇas* with *Siṁhalalāṭa*. In the early Chāḷukyan temples at Bikkavolu and Pondugula the *dēvakōṣṭas* are surmounted by *makaratōraṇas*. This element is absent in the temple at Avanigadda. Instead, *Siṁhamukhapati*, i.e., the lion's face is carved with protruding eyes and wide-opened mouth in the niches. The *Vyāla* figures are present on the *śikhara* part of the miniature shrines.

(7) The use of *citrakhaṇḍa* and *vyāla* type pillars in the temple with the expansion of *phalaka* in the abacus and the introduction of *padmabandha* between the shaft and the capital shows that they were in order of Chōḷa pillar and capital.

Thus the present study makes it clear that the Viṣṇu temple at Avanigadda was very much influenced by the later Chāḷukyan ideals and later Chōḷa architectural elements. It should be noted here, that the temple under study, which was constructed during the Chāḷukya Chōḷa rule in Āndhradēśa is the best example of the perfect blend of the Chāḷukya and the Chōḷa architectural styles.

NOTES AND REFERENCES

1. *S.I.I.*, Vol. IV, Nos. 943, 944, 945, 946.
2. *Ibid.*, No. 944.
3. *Ibid.*, No. 943.
4. V. Yasodadevi, "The History of Andhra Country 1000 A.D.—1500 A.D. (Subsidiary Dynasties), *J.A.H.R.S.*, Vol. XXVI, p. 72.
5. *S.I.I.*, Vol. IV, No. 1130 ; *Ibid.*, Vol. X, No. 151.
6. *Ibid.*, Vol. VI, Nos. 210, 211.
7. *Ep. Ind.*, Vol. IV, No. 4.
8. *Kēyūrabāhu Charitra*, Canto I, Verses 16, 18 and 19.
9. M. Rama Rao, *Select Andhra Temples*, Hyderabad, 1970.

10. M.A. Dhaky, *The Indian Temples in Karnatak Inscriptions and Architecture*, New Delhi, 1977, Figs. 2, 3, 4, 6, 8, 15, 22, 23.

11. *Marg*, Vol. XXXI, No. 1, "In Praise of Hoysala Art," pp. 47-56.

12. D. Hanumantha Rao, "The Sculptural Wealth of Sangamesvara Temple at Kudavalli, Alampur Taluk (Mahabubnagar District), *Itihas*, Vol. VIII, No. 1, pp. 44-65.

13. Douglass Barret, *Early Chōla Architecture and Sculpture*, p. 32.

14. Alexander Rea, *Pallava Architecture*, Pls. XVI, XVIII.

15. S.R. Balasubrahmanyam, *Early Chōḷa Temples, Parāntaka I to Rājarāja*, New Delhi, 1971, Pls. 32, 52, 56, 77, 92, 93, 104, 286.

16. K.V. Soundar Rajan, *Indian Temple Styles, the Personality of Hindu Architecture*, New Delhi, 1972, p. 71 ff.

17. Percy Brown, *Indian Architecture, Buddhist and Hindu Period*, Bombay, 1956, p. 84.

2

KĀMĒSVARA TEMPLE AT GALLAVALLI

Gallavalli is a small village situated about 15 kms. away from Rajam in Bobbili taluk of Vizianagaram District, A.P. At Gallavalli, the temple is dedicated to Śiva under the name Kāmēsvara, now locally known as Kāmaliṅgēsvara. The temple is similar to the Orissan style of temples in plan and construction. So far, no attempt has been made by the art-historians and art-critics to underline the importance of the art and architecture of this temple, though it is closely located to the temples of Nārāyaṇapuram, Jayati, and Sarapalli of Vizianagaram district[1] which show the Eastern Gāṅga patronage of temple art and architecture in northern Andhra. Hence in the present paper, it is aimed to study in detail the architectural and iconographical features that appear in the Śiva temple at Gallavalli which reflects the popular local styles, the royal patronage and to ascertain the data of its construction on its basis.

The Kāmēsvara temple facing east, rises to a height of about 10 mtrs. from the ground and is without any *antarāḷa* and *jagamōhana*. The *maṇḍapa* in front of the sanctum appears to be a later construction. But the image of seated *nandi* (20" high) in the present *maṇḍapa* appears to be an ancient one. The temple is built of soft-textured Khondalite, which can be obtained from the neighbouring places. Just like the temples of Mukhalingam and Bhubanesvar, it is observed that no cementing material was used in the construction of the temple. Large blocks of stones, neatly cut and dressed were placed one above another in their pre-determined positions and held by a system of balance.

The ground plan of the temple shows that the sanctum is square internally and stands on a *triratha* plan externally with a wide projection in the centre of its external faces. The elevation of the temple can be divided into three sections, the base (*bada*) including the wall portion, the tower (*gaṇḍi*) and the apex (*mastuka*). The *bada* consists of three mouldings resembling those of Parasuramesvar and Vaital Sisiresvar group of temples at Bhubanesvar and that of Madhukesvara temple at Mukhalingam. The base mouldings (Fig. 1) consist of three levels in which the topmost is square in section decorated with rectangular panels of sculptures ; the second level is undecorated and rounded in section ; finally, the lowest level also plain, is called *Khura* or hoof after which it is shaped. According to *Śilpa Prakāśa*, this type of temple is known as *rathāyukta*, with its base being widely projected in the centre.[2] The *jaṅgha* is decorated with three *dēva-kōshṭas* of which the central one is wider than the other two and are decorated with the figures of Gaṇeśa, Kārttikēya, Mahishāsuramardinī and the images of the *dikpālas*. The niches have a over-hanging eave at its top with the images.

The doorway of the sanctum is of *triśākha* variety, like those found in the temples of Sōmēsvara and Madhukēsvara of Mukhalingam with the floral motifs on it. The *dvārāpalas* are found at the bottom of the door-jambs and are carved in square niches. The two niches on the east wall contain the images of Pārvatī. The lintel of the doorway can be observed by climbing the *maṇḍapa*, which carries the figures of nine planets in a long row and Gajalakshmī beneath it.

The *śikhara* of the temple goes up straight for more than half of its height and then begins to curve inwards and is curvilinear. Like the early Orissan temples, the tower of Kāmēsvara temple has in the centre on each of its faces a well-projecting vertical band which is continued to the top from the base below. It is decorated with several *chaitya* arches, which diminishes in size as they go up. The wide *chaityas* at the bottom contain the cult images. Vertically the *gaṇḍi*, is divided into seven *bhūmi-baraṇḍis*, each of which is covered by a *bhūmi-āmla* moulding with fluted *āmlas* in the angles in the *kānika-pāga*. The *gaṇḍi* is divided into five *pāgas*, i.e., a central *rāha-pāga*, two-side *anūratha-pāgas* and two outer most *kānika-pāgas*. On top of the *bisama*, above the *gaṇḍi* are carved four *nandis* facing different directions. The *bēki* is capped by a heavy fluted *āmalaka* and *khapuri*. Inside the temple the sanctum has no ceiling but a corbelled roof, above which might have been constructed to relieve the heavy load over it. The *prāṇāla* is to be seen at the *kuṁbha* level of the base-mouldings to the north of the temple.

As regards to the sculptural art and the iconography of the temple, it shows all the characteristics of the medieval art. In the centre of the sanctum is found a linga on a rectangular *pānuvaṭṭam*. The *pārśva-dēvatas* are

Gaṇēśa, Kārttikēya and Mahishāsuramardinī. The niches on either side of the central niches contain the images of *dikpālas*. The *kōshṭas* are sculpted with narrative scenes from mythology. The floral designs and narrative panels are enclosed within dotted outlines and appears to be a local practice which is not found in any of the Orissan temples. Similar type of treatment of the niches can be seen in the Dibbhēsvara temple at Sarapalli in Vizianagaram District.

It is mentioned in the *Śilpa Prakāśa* that the architect should place the image of Gaṇēśa on the south side and Kārttikēya on the back wall of the temple and should be set into the wall.[3] The image of Gaṇēśa in the central niche on the south wall of the temple (Pl. 9) conforms to this description as well as to that of the iconographical features described in the *Brihatsaṁhita* and *Śaiva Agama* texts.[4] He is four-armed, seated on an *āsana* with his left leg folded and the right leg hanging down. The right hands carry rosary beads and elephant goad and the left hands sweet-meat and *paraśu*. He wears *Kirīṭa-mukuṭa* and the probiscus of the elephant-headed, pot bellied god is carved as touching the sweet-meat held by his left hand. The sacred thread and armlets are formed by snakes. Two flying *vidyādharas* carrying garlands in their hands can be seen on either side in the two top corners. The mount of the god, the mouse is carved as moving to the left with a long tail. Strings of bells are found as ornaments for the neck and ankles.

The central niche on the west wall of the temple contains the image of the two-armed youthful Kārttikēya carved almost in round which conform to the description given in the iconographic texts.[5] He is seated in *ardhaparyaṅka* pose on a stool, with his right foot resting on a peacock, his mount. He holds a *śakti* in his right hand and a *kukkuṭa* (a fowl) in his left, the head of which is broken. He wears pearl stringed *yajñōpavīta* and a beautiful *hāra*. The hair is arranged in such a way that the side ones fall over his shoulders. His body is covered by a garment up to above his knees and the folds of the drapery fall down from over the *āsana*. The peacock is carved with its tail, below the seat of the image and as looking towards its lord. The image under study with two arms appears to be the *sātvik* form of the god and represents him in *yōga bēra*. Generally in the north Indian images, Kārttikēya is shown either seated on his mount, or standing before the mount or riding and had either two or more than two hands and faces.[6]

The image of Mahishāsuramardinī on the north wall of the temple conforms to the descriptions given in the *Śilparatna* with slight variations.[7] The image is ten-handed and is shown in aggressive pose, where the three prongs of the *śūla* pierce the demon. Her right hands carry a sword, wheel, trident and a *vajra*, while her left hands carry a bow, *nāga*, a sword, battle-axe and her natural left hand presses down the upturned head of the demon. The sword in the upper right hand is held horizontally over the head of the goddess. She is carved as standing firmly on her left leg and her right leg is placed on the back of the demon. The demon holds a sword tightly in his hands. Here the demon is shown in animal form and a human demon emerges from the decapitated head of the creature. This feature is in contrast to the earlier examples of the depiction of the goddess wherein the demon below the feet of the deity is shown with a human body and a buffalo head. The goddess wears *kuṇḍalas*, jewelled armlets and *kaṭisūtra*.

The images of the *dikpālas* carved in the niches on the outer walls partially conforms to the descriptions laid in the *Brihatsaṁhita, Śilparatna Aṁsumadbhēdāgama, Suprabhēdāgama* and *Pūrvakāraṇāgama*. Agni, Nirṛti, Varuṇa, Vāyu, Īśāna and Kubēra are carved as standing with two hands and their respective mounts.

Though the figure of Agni carved in the south-eastern niche correspond to the descriptions laid in *Vishṇudharmōttara*,[8] it shows two-armed god standing in *samabhaṅga*, holding a rosary in his right hand and a water-vessel in his left. He has a beard, an angry stare, long waving flames emanating from his body, sacred thread and few ornaments. The lower garment hangs up to his ankles. His mount, goat is carved to his right side. To his left, is carved a dwarfish attendant holding flames in his right hand.

The image of Nirṛti, the god of evil carved in the south-western niche shows the *dikpāla* standing on the back of a man, who is prostrating on the ground holding the sword and shield tightly in his left hand. He wears a long *yajñōpavīta kaṭisūtra*, armlets and bracelets. He is adequately decorated with *ratna-kuṇḍalas*, *hāra* and *jaṭāmukuṭa*. To his right side is carved a male attendant holding a sword in one of his hands.

The image of Varuṇa, found in a niche on the western wall is carved as standing in a very graceful pose. It shows the *dikpāla* holding a looped noose by its end in his left hand which rests on his hip with a water-vessel in his right hand. He is decorated with jewelled head-gear, the *ratna-kuṇḍalas*, necklaces, pearl *yajñōpavita* and the waist girdle. An oval halo is carved around his head. Below the feet is depicted the wavy horizontal lines and a *makara* with its opened mouth behind his feet indicate the presence of Gaṅgā. To his right side is carved the miniature figure of his consort, Gaurī standing in *abhaṅga* pose carrying the stalk of a lotus flower in her left hand. The image described above is similar to the figure of

Varuṇa, of the Rājārāṇi temple of Bhubanesvar[9] and does not correspond to the descriptions laid down in *Vishṇudharmōttara*.

Vāyu, the lord of the north-west corner is described in the *Vishṇudharmōttara* as two-armed, his two hands holding the two ends of the scarf worn by him, his garment being inflated by wind. *Śilparatna* lays down that he has a flag in the left hand and the right hand should be in *varada mudra* with a stag mount.[10] The image of Vāyu carved in the niche to the north-west side partially corresponds to the descriptions given in *Śilparatna*. Here Vāyu is shown as two-armed, standing in the *abhaṅga* pose holding an *ankuśa* in the right hand and a flag in his left hand. He is decorated with *patrakuṇḍalas*, *kanṭha-māla*, long *yajñōpavīta* and bracelets. His lower garment is inflated by wind emphasising his swift motion. To his right is carved a standing attendant with stag head.

Curiously, Īśāna, the lord of the north-eastern quarter did not occupy his allotted position in the outer side of the sanctum, instead the image of Kubēra occupied its place. The image of Īśāna, on the northern wall of the temple corresponds well with the descriptions given in *Vishṇudharmōttara*.[11] In it, this *dikpāla* is called Gaurīsarva which is another name of *ardhanārīsvara* Śiva. This conjoint aspect of Śiva and Umā can be seen in the image of Īśāna. He is carved as standing, with two hands, the right hand holding water-vessel and the left hand resting on an indistinct long object. From top to the feet the two halves are clearly demarcated. A prominent breast is shown on the left half. The right half wears *jaṭāmukuṭa* while the hair on the left is arranged with a big knot at the top and is decorated with ornaments. He wears a single stranded *yajñōpavīta* and *kaṭisūtra*. He is shown with an oval halo round his head and a male attendant to his right side. In each of the two top corners a lotus is carved.

The image of Kubēra carved in the north-eastern niche conforms to the features described in *Amsumadbhēdāgama*.[12] It describes the god as two-armed, the hands being in *varada* and the left hand holding a club, having a sheep for his mount, attended by his consort and the two *nidhis*, *śaṅkha* and *padma* in the form of two powerful spirits. The image of Kubēra is carved as standing *abhaṅga* on a *padmapīṭha* with two hands the right hand in *varada mudra* and the left hand holding a *śakti*. He wears a long *yajñōpavīta* and *kaṭisūtra*. The lower garment is shown up to his thighs. The hair is held as in *kirīṭa mukuṭa* and the side ones falls over his shoulders. His mount, sheep is carved as standing facing right, to his right side. To his left is carved the powerful spirit, *śaṅkha nidhi*. Lotus flower is carved on the two top corners.

In addition to the images described above, the loose icons of Lākulīśa and Gaṇēśa are to be seen within the precincts of the temple. It appears that the cult images are carved on loose slabs and then fitted in the shallow niches in the walls. The decorative motifs and scroll-work patterns on the door-jamb and around the niches are drawn in Orissan tradition. The carving of the secular human figures and some of the sculptures on the walls of the temple are carved mostly in relief. Women engaged in dance, music and men in hunting and battles are proportionately and beautifully carved. The sculptors made a bold departure from convention and introduced many popular folk themes in their art. The graphic portrayal of the men and women returning from hunting and the warriors sculpted with a variety of dress, men riding on horsebacks meant to display the might and power of the Eastern Gāṅga empire. Further, the portrayal of the monkeys in action in a narrative manner around the *kōshṭa* containing the image of Vāyu leads one to suggest that delightful fables are drawn from the famous epics. Thus the icons as well as the sculptures of the temple not only catered the needs of religious minded people but also served to attract the common folk and the masses.

There is no foundation inscription referring to the construction of the Kāmēsvara temple. But two inscriptions of Anantavarma Chōḍa Gāṅga[13] (A.D. 1077-1147), are inscribed on the walls on either side of the entrance to the temple. Of them, one is dated in his 41st victorious regnal year and registers the gift of lamp by Viṭṭapa Nāyaka, a *kannaḍa mangali* to lord Kāmēsvara dēva of Gallavalli. Recently two sets of copper plate grants are recovered near to the temple complex. Of them, the plates with larger dimensions edited and published by mc[14] belongs to 11th Century A.D., while the other set is roughly three centuries earlier than this. The recovery of these two plates near the temple strengthens the idea that the area in which the temple was located was under the authority of the Gāṅga rulers of Kaliṅga. Probably it was under their patronage that the Śiva temple at Gallavalli had been constructed and maintained.

The architecture of the temple is the typical example of the *rēkha* deul of Orissa. The elevation of the wall portion and its tower bears close resemblance to the Sōmēsvara temple at Mukhalingam[15] and Muktēsvara temple at Bhubanesvar. The carving of the nine planets in a row on the lintel of the doorway of the sanctum and the figure of Gajalakshmī are similar to those of the Sōmēsvara temple of Mukhalingam. It has been observed by K.C. Panigrahi and J.N. Banerjea, by the Śiva temples of Bhubanesvar that only eight planets are shown in the earlier ones, while Kētu being a later addition. Further, *Vishṇudharmōttara* which belongs to 5th Century A.D. suggests the depiction of only eight planets, omitting Kētu.[16] The image of Kārttikēya is carved with a cock in his left hand on the west wall and the image of Gaṇēśa with his mount on the south wall suggests that it belongs to a later period. In carving the Mahishāsuramardinī image the demon below her feet is shown as a human demon that emerges from the animal form. K.C. Panigrahi suggests that this type of depiction is to be seen only in the later images.[17]

Thus on the basis of the study of the architecture, iconographic progression in the above said images, as well as the epigraphs of the temple, it can be concluded that the Kamesvara temple was built in the middle of 11th Century A.D. It may also be observed that the art and architectural traditions which are current in Orissa and Mukhalingam found their way into Gallavalli. The Gāṅgas of Kaliṅga seems to have been responsible to construct the temples of Orissan style in northern Andhra, as this area was included in the Kaliṅga region in ancient times.

NOTES AND REFERENCES

1. Vidya Dehejia, *Early Stone Temples of Orissa,* Delhi, 1979, pp. 133-134; *Telugu Samskriti,* Vol. I (revised edition), 1983, p. 810.
2. Boner Alice & Sadasiva Rath, *Śilpa Prakāśa of Rāmachandra Kaulāchāra,* Leiden, 1966, II, pp. 66-69.
3. *Ibid.*, II, Appendix C, pp. 92 ff.
4. T.A. Gopinatha Rao, *Elements of Hindu Iconography,* Vol. I, Pl. II, Appendix C, pp. 1-13.
5. According to the texts, he holds in one of his hands a spear or a trident and in the other a fruit or a cock. His mount, peacock accompanies him. T.A. Gopinatha Rao, *op. cit.* Appendix C, pp. 205-228.
6. U. Thakur, *Kārttikēya in Literature and Art : Some Aspects of Ancient Indian History and Culture,* New Delhi, 1974, pp. 244 ff.
7. In the *Śilparatna,* it is described that the goddess should have ten hands and should hold trident, sword, spear, wheel and bow in the right and in the left, the noose, goad, *khētaka,* battle-axe and bell.
8. He is described as bearded, four-armed, four-tusked, three-eyed, riding a chariot with smoke standard drawn by four parrots and driven by wind, having his consort, Svāhā, on his lap, holding flames, trident, and rosary in his hands. J.N. Banerjea, *Development of Hindu Iconography,* p. 524.
9. *Ibid.*, p. 527, Pl. XLV, Fig. 1.
10. *Ibid.*, p. 528.
11. *Ibid.*, p. 529.
12. *Ibid.*, p. 528.

13. *A.R.*, No. 369 and 370 of 1934-35, p. 42 ; *A.R.* 46 and 47 of 1976 ; See N. Ramesan and N. Mukunda Rao (Ed.), *Temple Inscriptions of Andhra Pradesh—Srikakulam District*, 1980, Vol. I, Nos. 415 and 416, p. 323.

14. M. Krishna Kumari, "Rājarāja Dēvēndravarmuni Yuddhapura Tāmraśāsanamu S' 998" *Bharati*, January, 1986, pp. 30-33.

15. B. Masthanaiah, *Temples of Mukhalingam*, pp. 107-108.

16. *Ashṭauvā tatra kartavya grahaḥkētu rivarjitaḥ*
Sūryaś-sukrah kujō rāhu sauris-chandrō budhō guruḥ
kramēṇānēna kartavyaṁ tatra rājan grahāṣṭakaṁ ||

17. Panigrahi, K.C., *Archaeological Remains at Bhubanesvar*, pp. 125-134. He points out that the earlier images of Gaṇēśa are without his mount, mouse while in later examples the mouse is present. In the case of Kārttikēya, the earlier images depict the god with just his peacock, while later examples include the cock. In the earlier examples of the Mahishāsuramardini images the demon is shown in fully animal form and in the later ones, a human demon emerges from the decapitated head of the creature.

3

SOME INTERESTING IMAGES FROM ELAMANCHILI

Elamanchili (Lat. 17°35′ N, Long. 82°55′ E), the headquarters of the taluk of the same name is a railway station on the Waltair-Vijayawada section ofthe South Central Railway. In 1984 June, I noticed some interesting group of sculptures in the precincts of the Vīrabhadrasvāmy temple of this village. These consists of *sapta mātṛikas*, Pārvatī, Gaṇēśa and Brahma. These are done in sandstone except the image of Varāhi. Some of these figures are placed in the small niches facing North and South of the Eastern gōpura. The images of Brahma and Gaṇēśa are placed in front of the temple within the *prākāra* enclosure. The image of Ċāmuṇḍa is noticed in front of the Visvēsvarasvāmi temple at Panchadhārla (Lat. 17°32′ N, Long. 82°55′ E) which is 10 km. North-east of Elamanchili. As the temple of Virabhadrasvāmy and its *gōpura* are completely renovated, except the *prākāra* wall, it is difficult to determine the architectural details of it and similarly the age of the temple. Unfortunately, we do not know exactly where these images originally came from. No information is forthcoming from the villagers on this point. As some of the *sapta mātṛika* group are coated with thick plaster, the details are not clear. Hence, only three of them are taken up for the present study.

In Andhra, at Yelleswaram, an early panel carved with seven figures of divine mothers shows two-armed female figures seated in a row.[1] In the Golingesvara temple of Bikkavolu,[2] the figures of *Kaumārī* and *Ċāmuṇḍā* are carved, as seated female figures with four hands and their mounts below, on the walls of the *mukhamaṇḍapa* and on that of the *garbha gṛha*. In the temples of Alampur, Chāḷukya-Bhīmavaram and Drākshārāma, all the *sapta mātṛka* images are found seated in a row with four hands and their characteristic weapons and mounts.[3] Outside Andhra Pradesh, the seated figures can be seen in the cave-temples of Ellora and Elephanta. In Karnataka, at Aihole they are carved as dancing and at Vadval[4] in Gujarat, they are shown as the standing figures in full stature. In the Madhukēsvara temple at Mukhalingam, the ancient capital city of the Eastern Gāṅgas, the *sapta mātṛkas* are carved on the doorway of the *garbha gṛha* of the *Khakhāra* shrine on the North *prākāra* wall, accompanied by *Gaṇēśa.* The *sapta mātṛka* temple at Velachcheri[6] of Chengleput district of Sundara Chōḷa, which is exclusive of its kind belongs to the early phase of the Chōḷa sculptural tradition. The seven divine mothers' sculpture notice at Dadapuram[7] in Tindivanam and Perukanchi in Walajapet taluk of North Arcot district of Tamilnadu speak of the Chōḷa tradition in carving the *sapta mātṛka* images. From the observations made in studying the images in Elamanchili and from the artistic evidences from the above said places one can draw the conclusion that the images are the characteristic products of the early Chāḷukyan and the Chōla traditions and can be assigned to the first half of the ninth Century A.D. or a little earlier.

According to the Hindu mythology[9] the *sapta mātṛkas* were created by lord Siva out of the flames of his mouth to assist him in a fight against the demon Andhakāsura, who, fortified with the boons he had received from *Brahma,* was troubling the *dēvas*. The *sapta mātṛkas* devoured all the blood spurted out from the demon's body, thus helping Śiva to put an end to the demon Andhakāsura. According to the *Māyāmata* the seven goodesses flanked by Vīrabhadra and Gaṇēśa should all be sitting, left leg folded, right pendant, and the lower left and right hands in *varada* and *abhaya mudras.*

All the images belonging to the *sapta mātṛka* group in Elamanchili have certain common features. They are seated on a pedestal, in *ardhaparyaṅka* pose with the left leg folded and the right leg pendant. The lower garment worn starts from just below the waist level and runs beyond the knees. Like the figures at Mukhalingam, which had either round or elliptical halo round the heads of the divinities, the images under study had an oval *prabhāvaḷi* round their heads. The images are four-handed except that of *Cāmuṇḍa* and Pārvatī, with various weapons and are adequately ornamented. The images are approximately 135 cms. in height and have been carved almost in round.

The image of *Brahmāni* is inserted into a niche of the modern *gōpura* of the Vīrabhadrasvāmi temple. She is seated in *ardhaparyaṅka* pose on a stool. This deity has three heads and four arms. In the back right hand, she holds *kamaṇḍalu* and *akṣamāla* and in the back left hand she holds noose (*pāśa*). The front right hand is in *abhaya* pose and the front left hand rests on the left knee holding a sacrificial laddle. At her bottom is carved a swan. The three heads were adorned with *karaṇḍa mukuṭa.* She wears ear ornaments, necklace with pearls, armlets, bracelets and anklets. The lower garment is tucked at a lower waist-level and comes down just below her knee level. An *yajñōpavīta* is seen from her upper left shoulder down to the right side of her lower waist level passing between her breasts.

The figure of *Māhēsvarī* has four arms and is seen seated in *ardhaparyaṅka* on a stool. This deity holds *śūla,* which is mounted on a small pike in the upper right hand, *aksamāla* in the upper left, keeps the lower right in *abhaya* and the lower left in *varada* pose above her left knee. Her head is adorned with *jaṭa mukuṭa* and the ears with *kuṇḍalas.* She wears pearl necklace, bracelet, anklets and *kaṭisūtra.* Her lower garment is seen below her waist level which runs beyond her knees. The oval shaped *prabhāvaḷi* round her head is also beautifully treated with striations radiating from the centre. Below her folded right leg is carved the bull seated, facing the left side.

The image of *Vārāhī* (Pl. 10) is done in black basalt stone. It has the face of a boar and wears on her head a *karaṇḍa mukuṭa* and is adorned with ornaments made of pearls and corals. She is seen seated on a pedestal in *ardhaparyaṅka* pose with four hands in *abhaya* and *varada mudras* respectively, whereas the upper right holds a *pāśa* and the object in the upper left hand is not clear. The *kēyūra* on her lower left hand is beautifully treated and she wears anklets and bracelets. A flowing cloth is shown by a wavy line over the chest in the *upavīta* fashion. The oval *prabhāvaḷi* round her head is treated with wavy horizontal lines. The lower garment is shown with its folds, being arranged at regular intervals. A buffalo, the vehicle of *Vārāhī* is carved below her, facing the left.

The image of *Cāmuṇḍa* (Pl. 11) is placed in front of the ruined temple of lord Visvēsvara in the village of Pañchadhārla. The image shows only two hands, the right hand is partly damaged and the left hand clasps her child seated on the lap. Unlike the usual *Cāmuṇḍa* representations elsewhere this image is not ferocious but has some grace of its own. The image is with *atiriktāṅga* or emaciated ribbed chest, prominent neck and the sunken eyes. She is shown with massive breasts unlike the usual *Cāmuṇḍa* images which are generally shown with pendulous, skinny breasts. She wears a long chain, which is not close to her neck and passes through the middle of her breasts which runs almost upto her navel. Due to the weathered state of the sculpture it is not clear whether it is *muṇḍāmala* or not. Her hair is arranged differently to the right side of her head in a fan like fashion. She wears big ear rings and the lower garment is firmly tucked at her lowest waist level, the hem lying in the centre is adorned with a flower like *Kaṭisūtra.* The wavy lines on her right thigh show the folds of her lower garment.

The image of Pārvatī (Pl. 12) is shown with single pair of arms, seated with the folded left leg and the right leg being placed close to the left leg. Her right hand holds the *nīlōtpala* in *kaṭaka hasta*, while the left hand hangs free in a *lōla* position. She wears a necklace and *kuṇḍalas*. She has a very pretty waist and rounded breasts, oval face and the facial features are not clear. Below her waist she wears a lower garment and folds of drapery fall on the left ankle. The oval shaped *prabhāvaḷi* round her head is decorated like lotus petals.

The elephant headed and pot-bellied image of Gaṇēśa is found seated on a *padmapīṭha* with a mouse below it facing the right side. The figure contains four hands. He folded his left leg and rests his folded right leg against the side of his belley. He holds *paraśu* in the upper right hand and *akṣamāla* in the upper left, *danta* in the lower right and the lower left hand is placed on the left knee holding a bowl of sweetmeats. The head is treated in the natural shape of the elephant head and is adorned with *karaṇḍa mukuṭa*. His probiscus is turned to the left and is seen lifting the *mōdakas*. He wears bracelets, armlets, necklace and decorated with ornaments on his shoulders.

The figure of the three-faced and four armed Brahma (Pl. 15) standing in *samabhaṅga* is found as a loose icon in the precincts of the temple. The lower right hand holds *akṣamāla* in *kartarīmukha* pose, and the lower left hand holds a vase. The upper right hand holds a *pustaka* and the object in the upper left hand is not clear. He wears a jewelled nēcklace, *kēyūras*, wristlets, anklets and *kaṭisūtra*. He wears a double stranded *yajñōpavīta*, running over the left hand and the lower part of his body is covered up to his thighs from his waist level. The folder drapery hangs down between the two thighs like a band. His three heads were adequately decked with *patra kuṇḍalas* and *jaṭā mukuṭas*. The three faces of the God blossom with a smile on the lips. Below him to the right, is seen the swan, the mount of Brahma. Like the early sculptures of Badami-Aihole region and the early Chōḷa images the beard is totally absent and Brahma is depicted as young with a slim body.

The *sapta mātṛka* images under study partially agree with the description of the images found in the iconographic texts like *Pūrvakāraṇāgama* and *Vishṇudhārmōttara*. However, in the description of the *sapta mātṛkas*, the iconographic texts differ in few points.[10] It is significant to note that the *Çāmuṇḍa* under study contains only two arms with a child on her left lap, thus showing an early tradition in its carving. The group of *sapta mātṛka* figures in the Brahmanical cave temples of Ellora are represented with child on their laps. In the Mukhalingam[11] and Bikkavolu[12] sculptures, the *Çāmuṇḍa* is represented as the fearful emaciated skeleton with dishevelled hair, protruding teeth, lean breasts, shrunken belly with a garland of skulls. In the Bikkavolu images corpse is shown as her mount, whereas it is absent at Mukhalingam. It is generally considered by the art-historians that the representation of *mātṛkas* as youthful goddesses can be considered as belonging relatively to an earlier period. Hence, the images under study may be assigned to a period slightly earlier than that of the images of Bikkavolu and Mukhalingam. The image of Brahma, who is carved as young with proportionate slim body, without beard might have been sculptured after the early Chōḷa images.[14] The image of Gaṇēsa agrees in all respects with the Eastern Chāḷukyan sculptures. The two handed sculpture of Pārvatī in the group of images under study would certainly points to an earlier date.

Thus it is evident by the present study that the images as Elamanchili may be assigned to the first half of 9th Century A.D. or slightly earlier. Iconographically the Chāḷukyan, Gāṅga and Chōḷa schools of art traditions can be seen on the Elamanchili sculptures.

NOTES AND REFERENCES

1. Nigam, M.L., *Sculptural Art of Andhra* (1980), p. 55.
2. Nageswara Rao, S., *The Temples of Bikkavolu* (Unpublished thesis, Andhra University, 1982), pp. 183-184 and Pls. 63, 64 and 65; C. Sivarama Murti, *Early Eastern Chāḷukyan Sculptures*, 1962, Pls. XXIV, (C), XXIX, pp. 47-59, The Golingsvara temple is assigned to Guṇaga Vijayāditya's (A.D. 848-891) reign period.
3. M. Rama Rao, *The Early Chāḷukyan Temples of Āndhradēsa*, 1964, pp. 3-11.
4. K.V. Soundararajan, *Glimpses of Indian Culture—Architecture, Art and Religion*, 1981, pp. 222-231.
5. B. Masthanaiah, *Temples of Mukhalingam*, 1978, pp. 89-90. In it the Madhukēsvara Temple is dated to the middle of 9th Century A.D., See p. 105.
6. S.R. Balasubrahmaniam, *Early Chōḷa Temples Parāntaka I to Rājarāja I*, 1971, pp. 145, 264.
7. B. Venkataraman, *Temple Art Under Chōḷa Queens*, 1976, p. 72.
8. S.T. Baskaran, "The Saptamatrikas of Perukanchi," *Lalitkala*, No. 17, pp. 14-17.
9. T.A. Gopinatha Rao, *Elements of Hindu Iconography*, Vol. I, Part II, p. 389.
10. It is stated in the *Śaivāgamas* that the goddess should possess four hands, holding a *kapāla* in one of the hands, and a *śūla* in another, the remaining two hands should be held in *abhaya* and *varada* poses. It is also stated that she wears *muṇḍamāla* as *yajñopavīta* with dishevelled hair on the mount *padma*. Further, *Vishṇudharmōttara* gives a different description. It is stated in it that *Cāmuṇḍa* should possess as many as 10 hands holding *mushla, kavacha, bana, ankūśa, khaḍga, khētaka, pāśa, dhanus, daṇḍa* and *paraśu* She has a ferocious face with open mouth and protruding busts, emaciated body and sunken eyes with the dead body as her mount. The *Pūrvakāraṇāgama* further adds that

she holds in one of her right hands a snake. (T.A. Gopinatha Rao, *op. cit.*, Appendix C, pp. 151-52).

11. B. Masthanaiah, *op. cit.*, pp. 89-90.
12. S. Nageswara Rao, *op. cit.*, pp. 183-184 ; C. Sivaramamurti, *Early Eastern Chāḷukyan Sculpture*, Pl. XXIV (e) and XXIX.
13. C. Sivaramamurti, "*Geographical and Chronological Factors in Indian Iconography, Ancient India,* Vol. 6, January 1950, pp. 33-35.
14. S.R. Balasubrahmanyam, *op. cit.*, Pl. No. XXXV.

4

AN UNPUBLISHED SCULPTURE OF ŚARABHĒŚA MŪRTI FROM DRĀKSHĀRĀMA

Drākshārāma is renowned as a Śaivite pilgrim centre and also as one of the *pañchārāma* shrines since medieval period of Āndhradēśa.[1] Drākshārāma is located at a distance of 6 km. from Ramachandrapuram, which is a taluk headquarter of East Godavari District of Andhra Pradesh. The temple built of local granite is surrounded by two spacious *prākāra* walls, pillared cloister with minor shrines and is in two storeys. Worship is made to the lofty *liṅga* (15′ high) in the upper storey as in the other *pañchārāma* shrines of the period.

This image is noticed on the shaft of a pillar of *nandi maṇḍapa*, which is in front of the central shrine on the upper floor of the Bhīmēsvara temple at Drākshārāma. Here, an attempt is made to discuss the iconographical features of the image and to identify it with one of the aspects of Śiva as *Saṁhāramūrti*, i.e., *Śarabhēśa-mūrti* or *Siṁhaghna-mūrti*.[2]

The image is executed on polished black granite pillar and shown in the act of attacking a human being. The figure is ten-armed, with two heads of a bird, with prominent beaks. Below the head portion, the image is carved as a male human being up to the waist level, with the neck ornaments and a long *yajñōpavīta*. From the waist level, the image is carved with the body of a lion, the long tail of which is curled to the right side. At the bottom, to the left side is executed a human being in a helpless position with his legs stretched out as the sharp claws of the five left legs of the lion are attacking on his body. The five right legs resembling those of lion firmly rests on the ground. The front right hand of the god holds a long *śūla*, which he pierces into the human being below him. The other hands hold a sword, *bāṇa*, *kapāla*, *chakra*, *dhanus*, a snake and *akshamāla*.

According to *Kāmikāgama*[3] the *Sarabhēśa-mūrti* should have eight arms, two wings, which should be uplifted. It requires that the body above the loins should be that of a lion which should be wearing upon its head a *kirīṭa-mukuṭa*. There should also be side tusks and is to be shown as carrying with two of his legs *Narasiṁha*, who should be represented in the form of a human being with the hands held in *añjalī mudra*. *Śrītattvanidhi*[4] mentions the image of Śarabhēśa in a different description. It requires the image to have thirty-two arms, in the right ones of which are to be found *vajra*, *mushṭi*, *abhaya*, *chakra*, *śakti*, *daṇḍa*, *ankuśa*, *khaḍga*, *khatvānga*, *paraśu*, *akshamāla*, a bone, *dhanus*, *musala* and *agni*. The left hands should keep the *pāśa*, *varada*, *gada*, *bāṇa*, *dhvaja*, another kind of sword, a snake, a lotus flower, *kapāla*, *pustaka*, *hala* and *mudgara* and one hand should be embracing Durgā.

The image under discussion is devoid of *kirīta mukuṭa* with two wings, and is ten handed. Unlike the descriptions of *Kāmikāgama*, which requires the image to have a lion's face with side tusks giving terrific appearance, the image of Drākshārāma is executed with two bird heads. In carving the image of Narasiṁha below, and the other attributes of the God, it tallies with the descriptions of *Kāmikāgama* and can well be identified with the *Śarabheśa* form of Śiva.

Of all the stone images of *Śarabhēśa*, so far reported, the one on the *prākāra* wall of the Srisailam temple (Andhra Pradesh) is closely resembling to the image under study.[5] Therein, the image is ten handed, two bird headed with prominent beaks, *kirīṭa mukuṭas* as head gear, and a number of neck ornaments. But here, the legs of the lion are not carved as attacking Narasiṁha, but as resting on the ground. Further, the body of the lion is carved in a stylised form. Two other images reported from Madras[6] and Dārāsuram[7] has a lion's face with two wings. The sculpture of *Śarabhēśa* noticed in the vicinity of Khuldābād, just above Ellora hills, dated to 11th Century A.D.[8] is different from the Drākshārāma image. In this the hands and the lower portion of the figure are missing. It contains three faces with well executed *jaṭā makuṭas*. The central and right side faces are pacific and the left side one seems to be of an animal, possibly of a lion.

The bronze image in the Śiva temple at Tribhuvanam in Tanjore district[9] is represented as having three legs, the body and face of the lion, a tail and four human arms ; in the right and upper hand is the *paraśu*, in the lower right are the *pāśa*, in the upper left one, the *mṛiga* and in the lower left one, agni. With the front leg, the God is stamping Narasiṁha, who is struggling with his eight arms.

A general description of the parallel images made above, reveal that they are carved either with a lion's face with *kirīṭa mukuṭa* or with that of a double headed eagle. In carving the image of Narasiṁha below, he is invariably carved as a human being in all the cases with two hands except in the case of the bronze image at Tribhuvanam. It is also clear that the sculptors of the early medieval period did not strictly adhere to the descriptions laid down in the iconographical texts.

In fixing the date of the image under study, we can safely rely on the date of the temple itself. Though the earliest record of the temple is datable to A.D. 1038,[10] on stylistic and architectural grounds, the temple can safely be assigned to the first half of 10th Century A.D.[11] The sectarian rivalries among the Śaivites and Vaishṇavites which started as early as 7-8th Centuries A.D. became apparent in the medieval period. Particularly, in the wake of the emergence of militant form of Śaivism-Vīraśaivism in Andhra, efforts were made to depict God Śiva as being superior to Vishṇu. In that process, the myth makers of Śaivism of the period, had invented a new form of Śiva image, i.e., Śarabhēśa punishing Narasiṁha. This could have been to satisfy the religious zeal of the Śaivite *bhaktas*, who wanted to elevate the position of lord Śiva in the minds of the people of the time. It is interesting to note that the temple of Drākshārāma which was under the patronage of the Chāḷukyas, Chāḷukya-Chōḷas since its beginning, had displayed the syncretic form of lord Śiva combining a bird, human and the beast in the form of Śarabha. This occurrence of the Śarabhēśa image is not without significance in the context of the influences from Tamil land. Similar images are also to be seen at Dārāsuram, Tribhuvanam, Chidambaram and Madras. This would speak of the close relationship the Chāḷukyan sculpture bears to the Chōḷa art during the medieval period.

Thus by comparing the iconographical features of the image with the descriptions laid down in the *Śilpa* texts, as well as by finding out some parallel images in South India, it may be suggested that the image at Drākshārāma may be assigned to Śarabhēśa-mūrti form of Śiva though some features like the absence of the lion's face with *kirīṭa makuṭa* and the two uplifted wings do not seem to go well with this identification. This image belonging to 10th Century A.D. displays the religious zeal of the Śaivites, which reflected in the art tradition.

NOTES AND REFERENCES

1. See for the temple legends and *sthala purāṇas*, N. Ramesan, *Temples and Legends of Andhra Pradesh*, Bharatiya Vidya Bhavan Series, Bombay, 1972, pp. 112-119.
2. According to mythological accounts, Śiva assumed the form of a Śarabha, an animal with two heads, two wings, eight legs of the lion with sharp claws and a long tail to

punish Narasimha, who continued to annoy the inhabitants of the Heaven even after having destroyed Hiraṇyakaśipu. Śarabha caught hold of Narasimha, and put on the skin of Narasimha, as his garment and affixed the head on his *makuṭa.* With this, Vishṇu was humbled and retired to Vaikunṭha. From then, Śiva came to be known as Śarabhēśamūrti or Siṁhagna-mūrti.

3. T.A. Gopinatha Rao, *Elements of Hindu Iconography*, Vol. II, Part I, pp. 172-74 ; *Ibid.*, Vol. II, Part II, p. 90.
4. *Ibid.*, p. 173.
5. K.C. Aryan, *Basis of Decorative Element in Indian Art*, Rekha Prakashan, 1981, Delhi, Pl. LXIII.
6. H. Krishna Sastri, *South Indian Images of Indian Gods and Goddesses*, p. 148.
7. C. Sivaramamurti, *The Chōḷa Temples—Thanjāvūr, Gangaikoṇḍa Chōḷapuram and Dārāsuram* (4th Ed., Delhi, 1984), p. 32 ; P.V. Jagadish Ayyar, *South Indian Shrines* (rev. edn., New Delhi, 1982), p. 574 ; C. Sivaramamurti, "Parallels and Opposites in Indian Iconography", *Journal of the Asiatic Society*, Letters, Vol. XXI, No. 2, 1955, pp. 79-95 ; Fig. 25.
8. T.V. Pathy, "A Rare Sculpture of Śarabhēśa-mūrti or Siṁhagna-mūrti," *Indian History Congress Proceedings of the Fortieth Session*, Waltair, 1979, pp. 1122-1124.
9. T.A. Gopinatha Rao, *op. cit.*, Vol. I, Introduction, Pl. E, Vol. II, Part I, p. 174.
10. *South Indian Inscriptions*, Vol. IV, No. 1132.
11. K.V. Soundar Rajan, *Indian Temple Styles : The Personality of Hindu Architecture* (Motilal Banarasi Das, Delhi, 1972), p. 45.

5

TRAIPURUSHA DĒVĀLAYA AT VALIVERU, GUNTUR DISTRICT, ANDHRA PRADESH

In Coastal Andhra region, monuments of the Eastern Chāḷukyas and the Chāḷukya-Chōḷas have not been completely enumerated, though several works have been made on the well-known and famous Śaivite shrines including the *pañchārāma* temples. So far, the art-historians have not paid due attention on the existence of the temples of *trikūṭa* plan in Coastal Andhra.

The triple cosmic functions of *sṛishṭi* (creation), *paripālana* (maintenance), and *saṁhāra* (destruction) are supposed to be represented by the three gods of the Hindu faith—Brahma, Vishṇu and Śiva. Probably, to house these three gods were constructed the temples of *trikūta* plan, in which three separate sanctums are placed on each of the three sides of a common hall, which is generally square in plan. It has only one common entrance and a porch in front of it. Each sanctum is provided with a tower like superstructure on the exterior. Scholars who worked earlier, on the problem of the *trikūṭa* plan of temples and *traipurusha-trikūṭa* cults have confined their studies mainly to the region of Telangana in Andhra Pradesh and Bijapur region in Karnataka.[1] Hence in the present paper, the Śiva temple at Valiveru in Tenali Taluk of Guntur District (A.P.) is taken up as a case study to determine the religious and architectural symbolism in relation to the iconographical pieces lodged in *dēva-kōshṭas* on the outer walls of the temple.

Valiveru, is a small village situated 6 km. away from Tenali. The Śiva temple at this village is an ancient one, though, it is now completely renovated and plastered. In the temple premises have been kept two pillars on which can be noticed five inscriptions.[2] It is known from these records that the temple of the village, Valiveru was termed as *Traipurushālaya* as well as

Svayaṁbhū dēvālaya and the village was an *agrahāra* village situated in Velanāḍu-6000, a sub-division of Karmarāshṭra.

The temple facing east, contains three sanctums and is without any *upapītha.* The wall-portion above the *adhishṭhāna* contains three niches. These *dēva-kōshṭhas* are not decorated like the other Chāḷukyan monuments. The superstructure above the three niches appears to have been renovated which warrants any generalisations on the basis of its three *śikharas.* The central shrine which is square in plan contains liṅga, preceded by a small *antarāla* (passage chamber) which opens into the pillared *maṇḍapa.* To the left, of the central shrine, is another sanctum facing South, which is similar in plan containing the image of goddess, Pārvatī. Before the shrine-room is an *antarāla* housing the images of standing Vārāhī and Lalitāṁba. To the right side of the sanctum is another shrine facing east without any *antarāla.* In it, Siva in the form of Vīrabhadra, in *samabhaṅga* pose with ten hands keep in them *śūla, chāmara,* sword, *dhanus* and the lower hand rests on a long sword. He wears *vṛitta kuṇḍalas,* which are touching his shoulders. He is wearing a garland of skulls and *yajñōpavīta* and is adorned with anklets and serpent armlets. His lower garment is hanging down beyond his knees. Round his *jaṭā mukuṭa* is carved the tongues of flames. To his right, is carved with standing figures of Daksha with a goat's head, two eyes, two horns and with hands in *añjalīmudra.* On the exterior walls of the temple can be seen the images of *Mahishāsuramardinī, Dattāttrēya* and *Vīrabhadra.*

The *Rūpamaṇḍana* gives description of Dattātrēya, an incarnation of all the three deities of Hindu trinity under the name of *Harihara pitāmaha.*[3] The worship of *Harihara pitāmaha*—a unified form of the trinities of Hindu faith, Brahma, Vishṇu and Śiva—was fairly popular in South India since 7th Century A.D. The oneness in essence of the apparent triple nature of the gods reflected as three separate deities, and his iconic representations were found at Bādāmi, Ajmer, Halebid and Khajurāhō.[4] The medieval inscriptions[5] of Andhra refer to the setting up of the images as well temples dedicated to lord Śiva in the name of *Trikōṭisvara* (*Trikōtīsvara* may be a corrupted form of *Trikūṭēśvara*—"Lord of the three peaks").

The image of *Harihara pitāmaha* (Pl. 13) in the temple under study, is unique in the sense that three gods are represented in one image. It represents a complete figure of a youth, six-armed, seated with the left leg folded and the right leg being raised in a *yōgin* posture. The prominent *yōga paṭṭa* fastens the waist and the upraised right leg, as in *Sōpāśraya* type of yogic *āsana.*[6] He holds in his right hands, *triśūla* with a long *daṇḍa, chakra* and *akshamāla.* His front right hand holding the *akshamāla* is held in *chinmudra* in the manner of giving exposition. His left hands carry *śankha*, *ḍamaru* and the front hand is rested on a water-vessel, which was kept over his left lap. He wears a long *yajñōpavīta* and *udarabandha*. The hair is arranged upwards as in *jaṭābhāra* type. His ears are long and are decorated with oval *kuṇḍalas*. His hands are decorated with bracelets and serpent armlets. The squattish face, with broad cheeks, nose and wide eye-brows, reflect deep meditation. Below him are carved, two female figures with smiling faces, probably the consorts of Śiva and Vishṇu. The attributes of this god closely corresponds to *Harihara pitāmaha* described in *Rūpamaṇḍana*.

The image of *Mahishāsuramardinī* is carved as standing with the right leg bent and placed on the back of a lion, while the left leg is placed on the Mahisha. The image is eight handed and holds *khaḍga*, *śaṅkha*, *chakra*, *bāna*, *ankuśa*, and *dhanus*. Her two front hands hold the *śūla* firmly and is piercing the body of the *rākshasa*. Her second left hand is holding the *Asura* in the act of destruction. At the bottom of the right side is her mount, lion. The goddess is adorned with a head gear at the back of which is *prabhāmaṇḍala*. She is decorated with *ratna-kuṇḍalas* in the ears, *kucha bandha* across the prominent breasts and other usual ornaments. Her face is expressive and is exquisitely modelled with short nose, thin lips, wide eyes and shapely eye-brows.

Another image of the north wall of the temple is that of Vīrabhadra with four arms. His head is covered with *jaṭā mukuṭa* and the fire is indicated by the flames carved behind his head. He wears a long *yajñōpavīta*, *udara bandha* and a garland of skulls. He carries in his right hands, a *bāṇa* and a sword. In his left hands, were a *dhanus* and his lower left hand rests on a long sword. To his right side is carved the image of Daksha with folded hands and two horns on his head. The image is bare-footed and the lower garment hangs beneath his knees.

It is curious to note from the inscriptions of the temple, that the lamp donations were made to the three gods, Brahma, Vishnu and Śiva separately in different periods of time. Of them, one record mentions *Sarvalōkāśraya Śrī Vishṇuvarḍhana Mahārāja* and his 41st regnal year, as well as S' 983 (A.D. 1043).[7] He can be identified with the eastern Chāḷukyan ruler of the time, i.e., Rājarāja Narēndra, whose accession took place in 1019-1020. The latest inscription at Valiveru is dated in Ś 1026 (A.D. 1104) which refers to the temple not as *Traipurushālaya*, but as *Svayambhūdēvālaya*. It appears from this, that in the 11th Century the temple was known as *traipurushālaya* (the temple of the three great beings) housing three gods and giving equal importance to all the gods, had been styled differently as

Svayaṁbhūdēva temple in the first half of 12th Century giving importance to Śiva only.

The study of the *trikūṭa* temples in Telangana reveals two distinct types—(1) That enshrines Śiva, Vishṇu and Sūrya oriented to the South, with an *upapītha,* (2) That enshrines three Śiva *liṅgas* oriented to the East, lacking an *upapīṭha.* In Karnataka, the *trikūṭa* plan was evolved towards the end of 7th Century A.D. and spread over Deccan in the following centuries. The *trikūṭa* temples possessing the three *liṅgas* in Telangaṅa of 12th and 13th Centuries were considered family memorial temples. Similarly, in Karnataka also, an earliest royal memorial shrine was noticed at Bhadra Nayakana Jalihal near Pattadakal. By the inscriptional evidence of the place, it was identified as a royal memorial shrine of Chāḷukya Vikramaditya II (A.D. 733-744).[9]

The *Traipurushālaya* at Valiveru shows that Sūrya is not associated in the triad of Gods and the temple, facing east is neither with an *upapītha* nor with the three *liṅgas* in the sanctums. Further, from the study of this temple, it appears that it is difficult to view the *trikūṭa* temples of coastal Andhra region, either as family memorials or as royal memorials. Though the *trikūṭa* type of temples are not as numerous as they are in Karnataka or in Telangana, it is evident by the present study that these religious and architectural traditions had been carried out in the early medieval period in coastal region of Andhra.

The images of Vīrabhadra sculptured on the walls are common from the 9th Century and are installed in the *dēva kōshṭas* from the later part of 10th Century.[10] In the earlier period are seen the four armed images of Vīrabhadra. But in the later period, eight armed or ten armed holding the *khaḍga, sūla, ḍamaru, paraśu,* bow and arrow etc., with the standing goat headed Daksha holding the hands in *añjalī mudra* on the left side, mostly in accordance with the *Bhāgavata Purāna*, the *Kāraṇāgama* and *Śrītattvanidhi* are the most common. Hence, the two images of Vīrabhadra in the temple under study are most probably of the last decades of 10th Century A.D. The *Traipurusha* temple might have been constructed to meet some religious and ideological functions of the times that could not be fulfilled by the single shrined temples. Further, the syncretic image of *Harihara pitāmaha* in the *dēva kōshtha* emphasise the religious syncretism that pervaded the Śiva worshippers, who were anxious to express the oneness of the Supreme lord as well as to portray his superiority in the expression of art.

NOTES AND REFERENCES

1. Phillip B. Wagner, "The Problem of the Trikūṭa in the Architecture of Early Medieval Telangana 11-13th Centuries A.D.," Paper presented in the *Society for South Indian Studies*, Tokyo, 1984 ; K.G. Krishnan, "Traipurusha Trikūṭa Cults in Karnataka," "*Quarterly Journal of the Mythic Society*, Bangalore, LV No. 2, July, 1964; Sundara, A., "Traipurusha Dēvālayas in Inscriptions and the Related Temples in Dharwad-Bijapur region : Their Implications" in F. Asher (Ed.), *Epigraphy and Art History*, New Delhi, 1984.
2. *S.I.I.*, Vol. X, Nos. 6, 8, 9, 61, 214, Pl. I.
3. T.A. Gopinatha Rao, *Elements of Hindu Iconography*, Vol. I, Part I, p. 255.
4. *Ibid.*, pp. 252-255 ; Pl. LXXII, Figs. 1 and 2 ; LXXIII, LXXIV ; Of the four images of Dattatreya described by T.A.G. Rao with illustrations, two of them, i.e., the one at Ajmere (Pl. LXXIV) and the other at Halebid (Pl. LXXII) were sculptured as the three deities, seated or standing side by side, respectively. Two other images of him at Bādāmi (Pl. LXXIII) and Ajmere (Pl. LXXII) were sculptured as a single image, seated in *padmāsana* or in standing posture and the triple nature of the god is indicated by the characteristic emblems or attributes, See also, Avasthi, R., *Khajurāhō Ki Dēva Pratimaen* (in Hindi), Agra, 1967, p. 27, fig. 8.
5. *S.I.I.*, Vol. X. Nos. 94, 104, 127.
6. T.A.G. Rao, *op. cit.*, p. 255.
7. *S.I.I.*, Vol. X, No. 8.
8. *Ibid.*, No. 61.
9. M.S. Nagaraja Rao and K.V. Ramesh, "A Royal Memorial to Chāḷukya Vikramāditya II," *Madhu-Recent Researches in Indian History*, Ed. M.S. Nagaraja Rao, Sri M.N. Deshpande, Festschrift, New Delhi, 1981, pp. 175-177.
10. A. Sundara, "A Unique Vīrabhadra Image from Mūlguṇḍ," *Śrīnidhi-Perspectives in Indian Archaeology, Art and Culture*, K.R. Srinivasan Festschrift, Madras, 1982, pp. 152-154.

6

ṚISHIS IN ART AND INSCRIPTIONS OF MEDIEVAL ANDHRA

The *ṛishis,* who are generally known for the embodiment of learning, self-control, sacrifice, understanding, innocence, universal love, with a feeling of goodwill to all living as well as non-living, are highly valued in Andhra region. The several images of the *ṛishis* carved on the temple walls and those found in the temple and the several references to them in the inscriptions point to show that the sages are enlightened by *Vēdic* knowledge and ennobled by penance. Here an attempt is made to analyse the aspect of the worship of the *ṛishi*s in Andhra on the basis of the inscriptional and iconographical evidence, which gives an idea about the ṛishi cult during the medieval period.

The sages are associated with sacred spots, rivers and temples in Āndhradēṣa. Particularly, in the regions where river Krishṇā and Gōdāvarī flows, several temples are associated with the names of the seers. In this region, many of the temples enshrining the *liṅga* form of Śiva, may be either the *parivāra* shrines or the main shrines are named after the sages like Agasthya, Yāmunīsvara, Mārkaṇḍēya, etc.[1] The river Gōdāvarī is associated with the name of the sage, Gautami, whose daughter is like Jahnavī, the daughter of sage Jahnu, that is Ganga according to the legend. The copper plate grant of Rājarāja Narēndra enumerates that the river, Saptagōdāvarī had Tulya, Ātrēya, Bhāradvāja, Gautamī, Vriddha Gautamī, Kauśikī and Vasishthā as its branches.[2] Two inscriptions at Kommūru[3] refer to the donations made to Agasthēsvara. An inscription at Nutekki[4] dated A.D. 1158, states that Pāṇḍyarāja built the temple and *maṇḍapa* for God Agasthēsvara of Guntur. Similarly, the Markaṇḍeyasvamy temple at Rajahmundry was popularly known after a great sage, who attained salvation through the grace of Śiva.

The Bhīmēsvara temple at Drākshārāma is closely associated with the *ṛishis*. According to *Bhīmēsvara purāṇamu*[5], the seven *ṛishis* brought the waters of the river Godavarī to Drākshārāma with the desire of bathing the *liṅga* at the time of its installation in the Bhīmēsvara temple. Though the flow of Gōdāvarī was interrupted due to the curse of sage Tulyabhāga, the seven *ṛishis* managed to take the flow of the waters underground up to Drākshārāma. Near the *pushkariṇi* in the eastern entrance, is found the carvings of seven *ṛishis* with Arundhatī.[6] The images are sculptured as standing in seven miniatures shrines with small beards and *jaṭa mukuta* on their heads. Along with them was sculptured Arundhatī, the consort of Vasishtha. In the *Taittirīya Araṇyaka*[7] she is mentioned as a star like the seven *ṛishis* and as the only one who takes the place with the principal seers.

It is clear from the *pūrṇāhuti mantra* that the seven *ṛishis* are the seven aspects of Agni, *sapta jihvāḥ* (the seven flames) and *sapta ṛishyāḥ* (the seven *ṛishis*).[8] More than the worship of Brahma, the *ṛishis* devoted themselves to the sun and the fire. In carving the image of Agni in the *dēva-kōshṭa* of the Kāmēsvara temple at Gallāvalli, he is shown as standing two-armed image holding a water-vessel and rosary in his hands as well as with the long waving flames emanating from his body.[9]

The controlling of senses when one is in the mood of penance is beautifully expressed in the scenes of Arjuna's penance on the pillars of the Bhīmēsvara temple at Drākshārāma. The sculpture of Arjuna centrally stationed amidst four blazing fires depicts him in the act of practicing rigorous asceticism. The sculpture represents him as seated in *padmāsana* with his hands in *añjalī mudra* and his hair as *jaṭas* falling to his left side, with his face lifted up, adorating the *liṅga* which was carved on his top. In another figure of the same place, Arjuna is shown (Fig. 2) standing on his left leg and the right leg is folded, with his hands joined above his head in *añjali* pose with *agnis* on four sides for obtaining boons from Śiva.

Not only the glory of *tāpasya* (and penance) is expressed in the stone medium, but also *svādhyāya* and *pravachana* (learning and imparting knowledge of the Vēdas). In the north-eastern corner niche on the east wall of the temple of Nakkala gudi at Bikkavolu is the figure of a sage and his disciple.[10] The sage seated on a *pīṭha* in *ardhaparyaṅka* pose holds an *akshamāla* in his left hand. To his left is seen a disciple standing and writing on the palm leaves, while the teacher looks on at him. Another sculpture of the same theme is observed on the north wall of the Vīrabhadra temple at Bikkavolu, in which the sage is seated cross-legged with a book in front of him and a seated disciple in the attitude of writing.[11] In this, the position of the pupil in the presence of the master (*guru*) is well represented as the disciple is shown sitting on a less elevated seat than his master.

Śiva as a Pāśupata teacher in the form of Lākulīśa is a favourite theme of the Kaliṅga sculptors. Because of the rarity of Lākulīśa images in Andhra, scholars like J.N. Banerjea, C. Sivaramamurty and R.S. Nagasvamy had expressed that "the Lākulīśa images, which are frequent in Orissa in the east, Gujarat and Kathiawar in the West are very seldom found in South India."[12] But recent researches have brought to light few Lākulīśa images, which indicate the worship of Śiva in the form of Lākulīśa in Andhra in the medieval temples beginning from seventh-eighth Century A.D.[13] These are noticed at Kūḍavelli Sangamēsvara temple (7th Century A.D.), in the Rāmaliṅgēsvara temple at Prātakōṭa in Kurnool District (7th Century A.D.) and at Siddhavatam in Cuddapah district (8-9th Century A.D.).[14] By this it is clear that the early medieval period witnessed an intensive revival in the worship of Śiva due to the influence of Lākulīśa and his disciples. It is interesting to note an image of Lākulīśa in one of the ruined Śiva temples in the fields at Bikkavolu.[15] In this Chāḷukyan sculpture of 9th Century A.D. he is carved as seated in *padmāsana* on a lotus. On either side of the long lotus stalk are carved the human figures. The front two hands are in the attitude of preaching and the back right hand holds an *akshamāla*. The *lakuṭa* or the long stick is held against his shoulders. The Lākuliśa images placed in the niches of the medieval temples suggest the purity of thought in the *parā vidya* that he vouchsafes to the *ṛishis*.

The Dakshiṇāmūrti aspect of Śiva is to emphasize the highest learning that imparts to the oldest seers, who were themselves repositories of learning. The images of Śiva as *vyākhyāna* and *jñāna* Dakshiṇāmūrti are housed in the temples of early Chāḷukyan period. At Alampur, in the Visva Brahma temple (early Chāḷukyan temple of 8th Century A.D.) in the upper portion of the South wall Śiva is represented as *vyākhyāna* Dakshiṇāmūrti.[16] He is carved as seated under a tree in *utkuṭikāsana* pose. The region below his waist and his four hands are broken. He wears a highly flowing *jaṭāmukuṭa* and is adequately decorated. He is surrounded by four disciples in various attitudes, in three-quarters profile, in the moods of reflection and supreme satisfaction. The sage to the left is expressive of the pensive mood in contrast to the other that reveals a state of enchantment. These sages may be identified with the four sages mentioned in the *Kāraṇāgama*, as Agastya, Paulastya, Visvāmitra, and Angīras.[17] Belonging to the same period, in the Rāmaliṅgēsvarasvāmy temple at Satyavōlu (early 8th Century A.D.), Śiva is shown as Jñāna Dakshiṇāmūrti.[18] In this, he is shown as seated in *utkuṭikāsana* on a high pedestal. His lower right hand is in *jñāna mudra* and the upper right hand as holding *sarpa*. He holds *nilōtpala* and *akshamāla* in his left hands. His *jaṭābhāra* is carved into snail curls. He is decorated with jewelled bands on his forehead and is adorned with *kēyūras*, *valayas*, *kaṭisūtra* and *nūpuras*. A coiled serpent, two lions and a deer are shown on the pedestal below him. In this earliest image of Śiva as *jñāna* Dakshiṇāmūrti, the sages are not carved.

In the Bhīmēsvara temple at Samalkot, of 9th Century A.D. Śiva is represented as vīṇādhara Dakshiṇāmūrti. In this form, he is the presiding deity over music, which leads to utmost concentration and even to *mōksha*. Vyākhyāna Dakshiṇāmūrti of the same place, with his hands in *chinmudra* represents the acme of the intellect and the supreme knowledge. In this context, it is noteworthy to consider the *Harihara pitāmaha* image in the Traipurushadēvālaya at Valiveru,[19] belonging to 11th Century A.D. In this, he is shown as seated on a pedestal. Of the six hands, the front two represent the *pitāmaha* aspect of the God in which he holds a rosary in his right, the fingers in *chinmudra* and the left hand rests on a water-vessel. He is bound to his waist by an *yōga paṭṭa* of *sōpāśraya* type which reveals that he is in *dhyāna* (meditation), and emphasizes concentration.

The temple records of Drākshārāma[20] refers to the establishment of *maṭhas* and *satrams* (rest-houses) like Tiruvīdhi *maṭha*, Āṇḍāri *maṭha*, Kulōttuṅga Chōḍa *satramu*, and Paḍumaṭi *satramu* which provides facilities for the seers to reside. The kings, officials as well as various persons gifted garden lands, wet lands, cows for feeding the ascetics and their disciples.[21] In some records of the place, it is specifically mentioned that provision has been made to feed the ascetics, who came from the other regions (*dēśāntara tapasulaku, paradēsi tapasulaku, nānādēsi āgatulaina tapasulaku*).[22]

Inscriptions of the medieval period often refers to the *gōtras* of the brahmins, which show that they were invariably associated with a number of great seers.[23] It appears from the records of the persons belonging to the *Teliki* community[24] that they were the *gōtrins* of the 1000 branches of the families which sprang from the sage Paulastya (*Paulastya sahasra śākhānvaya gōtrulu*). As Paulastya was the father of Kubēra, a *dikpāla*, as well as the lord of wealth they might have traced their descent from him. Thus from the epigraphs, it is clear that not only the *gōtras* of the brahmin caste are derived from the sages, but even the fourth caste people are trying to trace their lineage from the sages to ennoble themselves.

Thus the association of temples with the seers when viewed from the iconographic representations as well as the temple inscriptions reveals that the spirit of adoration of sages was very great in the medieval times in

Andhra and that people from all walks of life are intended to claim either descent from the well-known great sages or to be associated with the worship of the sages. Particularly, the carving of the figures of *Saptaṛshis* and Arundhatī at Drākshārāma the earliest representation of its kind reflects the great devotion of the people to the *ṛishis* during the medieval times.

NOTES AND REFERENCES

1. C. Sivaramamurti, *Early Eastern Chāḷukyan Sculpture,* Madras Government Museum, Bulletin, 1957, p. 34.
2. *Indian Antiquary,* Vol. XIV, p. 48 ff.
3. *South Indian Inscriptions,* Vol. X, Nos. 78, 81.
4. *Ibid.,* No. 144.
5. *Bhīmēsvāra purāṇamu,* Āsvasā, 4, pp. 77-83.
6. C. Sivaramamurti, *Ṛishis in Art and Literature,* Delhi, 1981, Pl. I ; Also see John E. Mitchiner, *Traditions of the Seven Ṛishis,* Delhi, 1982, pp. 79-134. In it, the author has discussed at length, the reasons for the formulation of two main lists of the group of seven *ṛishis* ; the *ṛishis* of the first main list are associated with the region north of the Vindhyas, while the *ṛishis* of the second main list are associated with the regions of southern India, Śri Lanka and Java. He expressed that the change in the two lists was brought about mainly by the members of particular Brahman *gōtras* between 100 B.C. and 200 A.D. He includes Bhṛigu, Angīras, Atri, Vasistha, Marīchi, Pulastya, Pulūha and Kratu in the second list.
7. *Taittrīya Āraṇyaka,* 3.9.2, Ed. with the contemporary of Sayana, R.L. Mitra, Calcutta, 1872.
8. C. Sivaramamurti, *op. cit,,* p. 225.
9. M. Krishna Murti, "Kāmēsvara Temple At Gallavalli," paper presented in the *Indian History and Culture Society,* Seminar organised by the National Museum, New Delhi, 1986.
10. S. Nageswara Rao, *The Temples of Bikkavolu,* Unpublished Ph.D. thesis, Andhra University, 1982, p. 126.
11. *Ibid.,* p. 127.
12. J.N. Banerjea, Development of Hindu Iconography, p. 465 ; C. Sivaramamurti, *Early Eastern Chāḷukyan Sculpture,* p. 30 ; R.S. Nagasvamy, "The Origin and Development of Saivism" in *Sankara Shanmata Souvenir,* Madras, 1969.
13. I.K. Sarma, *The Development of Early Śaivā Art and Architecture,* Delhi, 1982, pp. 84-87.
14. *Ibid.,* pp. 54, 56.
15. C. Sivaramamurti, *op. cit.,* pp. 49, 50, Pl. XIXb ; Also see his *Early Andhra Art and Iconography,* Hyderabad, 1979, pp. 13, Pl. 59.
16. B. Rejendra Prasad, "A Note on the Images of Siva as Vyākhyāna and Jñāna Forms of Dakshiṇamūrti from Ālampur and Satyavōlu", *Journal of Andhra Historical Research Society,* Vol. XXXV, Mallampalli Somasekhara Sarma Commemoration Volume, 1976, pp. 295-297, Pl. LV.

17. T.A. Gopinatha Rao, *Elements of Hindu Iconography*, Vol. II, Part I, Delhi, 1971, 2nd edition, pp. 274-284.
18. B. Rajendra Prasad, *op. cit.*, Pl. LVI.
19. M. Krishna Kumari, "Traipurusha dēvālaya at Valiveru, Guntur District, A.P.", paper presented in the *Xth Andhra Pradesh Historical Congress*. 1986 ; *Bharati*, November, 1986, Pl. XXII, p. 24.
20. *S.I.I.*, Vol. IV, Nos. 1015, 1016, 1054, 1098, 1102, 1104.
21. *Ibid.*
22. *Ibid.*, Nos. 1102, 1104, 1248.
23. *Ibid.*, Nos. 1040, 1067, 1316 ; *Epigraphia Indica*, Vol. V, No. 10.
24. *Ibid.*, No. 668, *Ep. Ind.*, Vol. VI, No. 35, v. 38.

7

A SCULPTURE OF PAÑCHĀNANA ŚIVA FROM AVANIGADDA, ANDHRA PRADESH

Avanigadda, a small village in (Divi taluk, Krishna District) Andhra Pradesh is situated on the bank of the river Krishṇā. On account of the known antiquity of the Chōḍanārāyaṇa temple (now locally known as the Lakshminarayanasvamy temple) from the epigraphical data of the temple itself, a thorough exploration has been made by the author to find some traces of the sculptures and icons of the medieval times. Of the observed sculptures, the *pañchānana* Śiva is found to be very interesting and is chosen for the present study, as very few stone images of this aspect of Śiva are noticed so far, in Eastern Deccan. Hence an attempt is made in the present paper, to identify the sculptures of the five-faced seated image with the *Sadāśiva mūrti* form of Śiva and to discuss its philosophic aspect.

A beautiful sculpture of *pañchānana* Śiva is observed (Pl. 8) on the outer wall of the Eastern *gōpura* of the temple at Avanigadda. The sculpture is found in the *dēva-kōshṭha* of the outer wall of the *gōpura*, which was flanked by two slender pilasters and a *drāviḍa śikhara* at its top. The temple is a good example of the art and architecture of the Velanāṭi Chōḍas, who were the masters of the Velanāḍu region in Coastal Andhra, during the medieval period.

The sculpture of Śiva is carved on red sandstone, which measures 86 × 86 cms. The deity is carved as being seated on a pedestal in *ardhaparyaṅka* pose. The five heads of the image are arranged in one-tier and on the forehead of the central face, the third eye is shown. The five faces of the image are decorated with the *kirīṭa makuṭas*. The deity is profusely ornamented. He is decorated with ear ornaments, *kanṭha māla, nāga kēyūras*, *kaḍiyams*, and *nūpuras*. He is adorned with *udarabandha* and *yajñōpavīta*.

The under-garment is shown over the knees and adds beauty to the sculpture. The image has ten arms, five on each side. The front right hand is in *abhaya mudra* and the left hand in *vyākhyāna mudra.*[1] In the other hands, only *ḍamaru, triśūla* and *kamaṇḍalu* can be seen. The rest of the details about the weapons in the other hands cannot be made out as they are partly damaged.

According to the Śaiva *Āgamas,* the five faces of *Sadāśiva* represent *Tatpurusha, Aghōra, Vāmadēva, Sadyōjāṭa* and *Īśāna,* collectively known as *Pañcha Brahman* and regarded as the emanations from the formless (*Nishkala*) Śiva.[2] These five heads of Śiva symbolise the soul, material world, *buddhi, ahaṁkāra* and the mind.[3] In the *Vishṇudharmōttara purāṇa* (datable to 6th Century A.D.) the iconography of the *Sadyōjātādi mantra svarūpas* is found.[4] The five aspects of Śiva are mentioned in the list of *ekādaśa Rudras* in a later work, *Aparājitaprichcha.* Although the position of each face is not specified, Kāraṇāgama also refers to five faced Śiva *liṅgas* by the epithet, '*Sarānanaṁ*'. The *Rūpamaṇḍana* (an iconographic text of 15th Century A.D.) also gives interesting details about the *mukhaliṅgas.* It has been stated that the fifth face Īśāna, is beyond the ken even of the *yōgis.*[5]

The *Uttara Kāmikāgama* states that the colour of *Sadāśivamūrti* should be of white and be standing upon a *padmāsana.* There should be five faces and the heads be adorned with *jaṭāmakuṭas,* whose *jaṭas* are required to be of brown colour. *Sadāśiva* should have ten arms. In the five right hands, there should be the *śakti, śūla, khaṭvāṅga, abhaya, prasāda* and in five left ones, the *bhujaṅga, ḍamaru, nilōtpala* and a fruit of *mātuluṅga.*[6] But in the *Vishṇudharmōttra,* it has been stated that the ten arms should keep in their hands the *khaḍga, khēṭaka, dhanus, bāṇa, kamaṇḍalu, akshamāla, varada, abhaya, śūla* and *padma.*[7]

During the early medieval period, certain new iconographic forms of gods and goddesses were evolved. The icons of Śiva in composite forms were first produced only in Deccan.[8] At Virinchipuram in North Arcot district, is observed a good specimen of *pañchamukhaliṅga.*[9] On the *rudra-bhāga* of the *liṅga* has been carved the five faces up to the neck. Four of them, were facing the cardinal directions, while the fifth one is facing up-wards. The recovery of the *chaturmukhaliṅga* from Amarāvati, assignable to the Sātavāhana workmanship[10] indicate the prevalence of *Sadāśiva tattva* in Andhra during the first-second Centuries A.D. It appears that the ideology underlying the *chaturmukhaliṅga* was later transformed into a human physical form. This made the artist of the medieval period, to carve the deity with five heads and ten arms holding different attributes.

In the early iconographic representations of *Sadāśivamūrti* aspect of Śiva, only the *mukhas* are extant and are carved on the *rudrabhāga* of the *liṅga* forms. But it appears that, in the later times, the full physical form, was carved as per the *āgama* rules. An image of *Sadāśivamūrti*, datable to 9th Century A.D. is reported from Kaveripakkam in North Arcot District.[11] The image holds *ḍamaru*, a sword, a trident and one hand in *abhaya* pose and the rest of the arms are broken. Recently, an image of *ēkādaśā Rudra* from Pedda Vēgi datable to 6-7th Centuries A.D. of Vishṇukuṇḍin workmanship has been published.[12] Previously, it was considered as an unique sculpture of *Mahā Sadāśiva* with ten heads, and twenty arms and is assigned to a period of about 13th Century A.D.[13] But now, this view has been reasonably questioned by I.K. Sarma, who projects this icon as a form of *ēkādaśa rudra* with eleven hands and twenty-four arms. It is standing image made on red sandstone, with all the Śaivite weapons and attributes in its twenty-four arms.[14] This image of the early medieval times, represents, how *Rudra* has been divided into eleven minor Rudras, collectively known as *ēkādaśa rudras* from the frown of Brahma on the stone media.

The occurrence, date and the iconographic features of the *Sadāśivamūrti* forms of Śiva stated above, reveal that *Sadāśiva* worship in the eastern Deccan has an early beginning. The *pañchānana* image of Śiva under study, tallies with the descriptions laid down in the *Vishṇudharōttara purāṇa.* The three eyes shown on the central face of the image represents the sun, the moon and the fire. The sculpture showing the continuation of the Vishṇukuṇḍin tradition of carving multi-faced Śiva in the Chāḷukya-Chōḷa period, can be dated to the first half of 12th Century A.D.

Though the iconographic features of *Sadāśiva* in human form have been described in the *Vishṇudharmōttara purāṇa*, the artists do not seem to have preferred it much. Instead, *Sadāśiva* was mostly represented in Andhra by the *chaturmukhaliṅgas* with a rounded dome suggesting him Īśāna aspect.[15] In this respect, the present study is significant, as it has brought to light a hitherto unnoticed image of *Sadāśiva* with five faces, of 12th Century A.D. in the Coastal Andhra region.

NOTES AND REFERENCES

1. *Vyākhyāna mudra* is also known an *jñāna-mudra*, i.e. joining the tips of the thumb and the index finger and straightening the other fingers after joining them together.
2. T.A.G. Rao, *Elements of Hindu Iconography*, Vol. II, Part II (2nd edn., Varanasi, 1971), p. 371.
3. Agrawala, V.S., Śiva Mahādēva, *The Great God, An Exposition of the Symbolism of Śiva* (Varanasi, 1966), pp. 18-20.

4. Priyabola Shah (Ed.), *Vishṇudharmōttarapurāṇa*, III, Kanda, Intro., P. XXVI, GOS No. XXX (Baroda, 1958, 1961).
5. B.N. Sharma, *Iconography of Sadāśiva* (Delhi, 1976), p. 3.
6. T.A.G. Rao, *op. cit.*, Vol. II, Pl. II, p. 375.
7. *Vishṇudharmōttarapurāṇa*, III, 48, 1-19.
8. Rahman Ali, "A Unique Sculpture of Sadāśiva," *Indian Archaeology—New Perspectives* (Ed.), R.K. Sharma, Delhi, 1982, pp. 308-310.
9. I.K. Sharma, *Development of Early Śaiva Art and Architecture*, Delhi, 1982, p. 81.
10. I.K. Sharma, "Chaturmukhaliṅga from Amarāvati", *Bharati*, November, 1980, pp. 53-57.
11. B.N. Sharma, *op. cit.*, Pl. III, p. 4.
12. I.K. Sharma, " Āndhrula Prāchīna Nagaramu Pedda Vēgi : Ichchati Puravastu Parisodhanalu," *Bharati*, Jan., 1987, Pl. XIII, pp. 3-9.
13. K. Krishna Murty, "A Unique Sculpture of Mahāsadāśiva from Pedda Vēṅgī, Andhra Pradesh", *Journal of Oriental Research*, XXXVI, I-IV, pp. 1-2 ; B.N. Sharma, *op. cit.*, Pl. XXX, p. 21.
14. I.K. Sharma, *op. cit.*
15. I.K. Sharma, *The Development of Early Śaiva Art and Architecture*, pp. 74-92.

8

ICONOMETRIC ANALYSIS OF THE IMAGES OF BHĪMESVARA TEMPLE AT CHĀLUKYA BHĪMAVARAM (SAMALKOT), ANDHRA PRADESH

In the eastern Deccan, a new conception of temple building activity has been started from the reign of Chāḷukya Bhīma I (A.D. 892-922), an Eastern Chāḷukyan king. Although none of his inscriptions during his life time allude to his achievement of the grand temple building activity, a few inscriptions of late period credits him as the founder of Chāḷukya Bhīmēsvara temple in Kumārārāma.[1] A recently noticed sculptural panel[2] representing the figures of king Chāḷukya Bhīma I and his wife lends support to the view that Chāḷukya Bhīma was the founder of the Śiva temple named as Kumārārāma Bhīmēsvara at Chāḷukya Bhīmavaram. In the present paper, an attempt is made to analyse the iconometry of the sculptures of the temple of Chāḷukya Bhīmavaram with the application of statistical methods and to compare them with the descriptions laid down in the *Śilpa* texts. It is also aimed to discuss the range of variation in iconometric proportions and hypothesize the characteristics of the sculptures of Chāḷukya Bhīma I's period in terms of the sculptural proportions. This will enable one to search for the parallel sculptural portions in the other *pañchārāma* shrines, which are said to have been constructed during his reign period.[3]

The Bhīmesvara temple (24.6×13.9 m) is a two storeyed structure enclosed by two *prākāras* and a pillared cloister. The pillared *maṇḍapa* around the temple contains several niches which contains the seated images of dakshiṇāmūrti, caṇḍēśa, vīṇādhara dakshiṇāmūrti, saptamātṛikas and the standing images like dvārapālas, Sūrya, Dattātrēya, Kārtikēya, Vishṇu and Vīrabhadra. Though the iconographical features of these images have already been reported,[4] so far no attempt has been made by the scholars to study the iconometry of these sculptures. Some scholars generally believe that the Chāḷukyan sculptures were influenced by Indian canons of iconometry. Hence, an attempt is made to test such a theory by comparing the canonical descriptions with the actual measurements.

All the images of the Bhīmēsvara temple considered here are the sculptures in round and are either in the standing or seated postures. To compare the different figures in various stances, their facial measurements are taken using the sliding and spreading calipers and following the principles of anthropometry.[5] Particularly ten facial proportions such as nose length, nose breadth, eye length, eye breadth, lip length, lip breadth, face length, face breadth, length of the face excluding the width of the forehead and the distance from nose to chin are considered in this study.

All the *Śilpa* texts prescribe that the face length should be equally divided by the width of the forehead, length of nose and distance from nose to chin. The *Śilpa* texts prescribe that the length of the face should be 12 *aṅgulas*, and they also prescribe the length and breadth of the nose, eyes and lips in *aṅgula* measurements.[6] For this reason, the actual measurements taken of the sculptures were converted to *aṅgula* units by dividing by face length and multiplied by 12. The average values of measurements made on sculptures of the Bhīmēsvara temple and the canonical values of facial proportions prescribed in the *Śilparatna* are given in Table 1. These values give us the standard proportions used by the sculptors of the Bhīmēsvara temple.

Considering the variations among the facial proportions, these measurements were subjected to chi-square test,[7] to determine whether, or not, the Chāḷukya sculptors had followed the principles laid down in the *Śilpa* texts in carving out the sculptures. The test so conducted revealed no significant differences between the expected (scriptural) measurements and the actual (observed) measurements of the various facial parts of the icons (Table 1).

It is interesting to note that the sculptures of the Bhīmēsvara temple have longer and wider noses and longer eye length than those prescribed by the canons. It is further interesting to compare the facial measurements of the images under study with those of the Dharmarāja *ratha* at Mahābalipuram (7th Century A.D.) and Kailasanatha temple (8th Century A.D.).[8] (See Table 2 for details).

TABLE 1

Canonical values of facial proportions from Silparatna and average values of measurements made on the sculptures of Chāḷukya Bhīmavaram (N=10)

Sl. No.	Variables	Śilparatna canons	Chāḷukya Bhīmavaram temple
1.	Face length	12.00	12.00
2.	Top of the nose to chin	8.00	8.51
3.	Nose length	4.00	4.71
4.	Nose to chin	4.00	3.81
5.	Nose breadth	1.00	3.62
6.	Eye length	2.00	3.95
7.	Eye breadth	2.00	1.80
8.	Lip length	4.00	4.32
9.	Lip height	2.00	1.46
10.	Face breadth	12.00	10.21
	Sample size	—	16

d.f.=9 ; X^2=9.3 significant at both 1 per cent and 5 per cent levels.

TABLE 2

Canonical values of facial proportions from Śilparatna and average values of measurements made on sculptures of Chāḷukya Bhīmavaram temple, Dharmarājaratha and Kailāsanātha temple (in aṅgulas)

Sl. No.	Variables	Śilparatna canons	Chāḷukya Bhīmavaram temple	Dharmarāja *ratha*	Kailāsanātha temple
1.	Face length	12.00	12.00	12.00	12.00
2.	Top of the nose to chin	8.00	8.51	8.95	9.00
3.	Nose length	4.00	4.71	4.78	5.40
4.	Nose to chin	4.00	3.81	4.19	3.61
5.	Nose breadth	1.00	3.62	3.21	3.57
6.	Eye length	2.00	3.95	2.39	3.41
7.	Eye breadth	2.00	1.80	1.01	0.79
8.	Lip length	4.00	4.32	3.47	4.30
9.	Lip height	2.00	1.46	1.54	1.75
10.	Face breadth	12.00	10.21	10.45	11.11
	Sample size	—	16	52	39

The above table shows that the sculptures of Chāḷukya Bhīma I's period had longer noses (4.6 *aṅgulas*) than those prescribed in the *Śilpa* texts (4 *aṅgulas*) and not as long as the noses of Rājasiṁha period (5.4 *aṅgulas*). As regards to the nose breadth and eye length, it is longer than that mentioned in the canonical texts and this appears to be somewhat similar with those of the Pallava sculptures. The face breadth of the Chāḷukya Bhīma sculptures is less than the canonical descriptions and is somewhat similar to those of Dharmarāja *ratha* sculptures and is different from the Kailāsanātha sculptures. Thus the sculptures of Chāḷukya Bhīma I's period are different from those of the Pallava sculptures of 7-8th Centuries A.D. although there is no significant variation between them and the iconographic measurements mentioned in the *Śilpa* texts. From this, it can be stated that the sculptors of the Chāḷukyan period had neither strictly followed the facial proportions mentioned in the *Śilpa* texts, nor those followed by the *Pallava* sculptors of Dharmarāja *ratha* or Kailāsanātha temple.

To determine whether the same kind of sculptures were executed Drākshārāma in the Bhīmēsvara temple, which is also attributed to the period of Chāḷukya Bhīma I, an intensive study has been made by the author on its sculptures. But it is found difficult to carry out the iconometric analysis on them, as there are very few sculptures in relief and moreover, their facial features are badly damaged.

It is found that the iconographical features of Mahishasuramardinī, Brahma, Vīrabhadra and *saptamātṛikas* generally agrees with those of the Bhīmēsvara temple at Chāḷukya Bhīmavaram. However, it is significant to note that the iconometric proportions of the sculptures of the Chāḷukya Bhīma's temple are not found in the rest of the *Pañchārāma* shrines, i.e., Drākshārāma, Pālakollu, Amarāvati and Bhīmavaram. Thus, the iconometric evidence of the Bhīmēsvara shrines shows that all the *Pañchārāma* shrines do not belong to the same period.

NOTES AND REFERENCES

1. *Epigraphia Indica*, Vol. IV, pp. 226-242 ; M. Sambasiva Murthy, "Edarupalli Re-issued Copper Plate Grant," *Bharati*, Jan., 1968, p. 3.
2. D. Dasaradhi, "A Sculptural Representation of Chāḷukya Bhīma I," *Andhra Pradesh History Congress Proceedings of the Ninth Session*, Kurnool, 1985, pp. 52-57.
3. *S.I.I.*, Vol. VI, No. 665.
4. M. Rama Rao, *Eastern Ch.ḷukyan Temples of Āndhradēśa*, (Hyderabad, 1964) ; B. Rajendra Prasad, *Art of South India : Andhra Pradesh* (Delhi, 1980), p. 128.

5. I.P. Singh, Bhasin, M.K., *Anthropometry* (Delhi, 1968).
6. N. Devanthachari (Ed.), *Śilparatna* (1961) ; Subrahmanya Sastry, K.S. (Ed.), *Kāśyapa Śilpaśāstram* (1960), Saraswati Mahal Library, Tanjore.
7. I.P. Singh, Bhasin, M.K., *op. cit.*, pp. 213-221.
8. Gift Siromoney, M. Bhagavandas and S. Govindaraju, "Iconometric Analysis of the Dharmarāja *ratha*," *Śrīnidhi-Perspectives in Indian Archaeology, Art and Culture* (Madras, 1983), pp. 137-150 ; Also see Gift Siromoney *et al.*, "Temple Carvings of Southern India," *Perspectives in Computing*, Vol. 5, No. 1, Spring, 1985, pp. 34-43.

GLOSSARY

abhaṅga	posture of an archer
abhaya mudra	a hand posture to convey assurance. The pose consists in holding the hand up with the palm showing up
āchāri	a suffix usually found in the names of the scribes of the records or the members of the *Viśvakarma* community
adhikāri	superintendent
adhishṭhāna	Base ; plinth part, below the wall portion. It is first among the six parts and consists of moulded tiers, each having distinct name like—*upāna*, *jagati*, *kumuda*, *kanṭha*, *kampa*, and *paṭṭika*. The crown part is generally a cornice or *kapōta* with *kūḍus*
agrahāra	land or village gifted to brahmins free of all taxes
akshamāla	a chain of rosary beads
āmla	ribbed, flattened, spheroid structure set above the *bēki* in *rēkha* temple
amudu	food offering made to god
añjalī mudra	hands folded in reverence
ankuśa	elephant-goad
antarāḷa	ribbed, flattened, spheroid structure set above the *bēki* in *rēkha* temple
antarāya	tax on land
anūratha pāga	second *pāga*
archana	religious service

ardhaparyaṅka	a seated posture in which one leg (left) is tucked upon a seat, while the other (right) is dangling
āsana	a seat
bāṇa	an arrow
bēki	position between *bisama* and *āmla* of *rēkha* temple
bhaṇḍāri	officer-in-charge of the temple treasury
bhaṭṭāra	a noble lord
Bhūmi	plane, planes into which the body of a temple is divided
bhūmi-baraṇḍis	all mouldings in *bhūmi* of *kānika paga* except the *bhūmi* amla in *rēkha* temple
brahmādēya	gift to brahmins, especially a village or land to brahmins for their maintenance
chaturvēdi-mangalam	an *agrahāra* village donated to the brahmins, generally named after the donor of the grant
chinmudra	hand in the attitude of exposition
daṇḍanāyaka	a general ; a leader of forces, an army officer ; a military commander
deul	the sanctum of a temple
dēvadāna	a village or land granted to a Hindu temple
dēvakanmi	a temple officer
dēvakōshṭha	niches on the walls containing shrines of divinities
dikpālas	The guardian angels at the four cardinal and four intermediate points of the compass
gaṇḍi	between *bada* and *bisama*
garbha gṛiha	the womb-chamber ; the inner-most sanctuary of the temple
gōpura	tower-like structure in front or on the cardinal directions of the temple with an entrance
gōtra	a sect ; a clan
hāra	string of shrine miniatures that runs over the parapet

	of each *tala* and comprising *kūṭas* at the corners and *sālas* in between
jagamōhana	structure in front of *rēkha*
jagati	a form in southern temples at the base of the *adhishṭhāna* above the *upāna*
jangha	wall part of a temple
jaṭābhāra	a clustered hair over the head
kalaśa	vase like member crowning a Śiva temple
kamaṇḍalu	same in *kuṇḍika* with two openings carried by deities and rishis
kānika pāga	outer-most segment on the face of the temple
Kaṅkāni	an overseer, supervisor or a superintendent of the temple
kanṭha	neck-moulding
karaṇḍa mukuṭa	crown decorated with *karaṇḍas* or series of flattish pots
kartari	curved, sharp knife
kaṭi sūtra	girdle ornament or rope
kēyūra	armlet, a flat ornament worn on the arm
khakhāra	temple with a barrel vaulted tower
khapuri	structure resembling flattened bell on *āmla*
khura	the lowest section of base-moulding shaped as a hoof
kulastree	a lady of a respectable family
kuṁbha	water-pot, similar mould used in *pābhāga*
kuncham	a grain measure
kuṇḍala	an ear-ring
kūṭa	a *Śikhara* unit
liṅga	phallic emblem of Śiva
māḍas	type of Coins
Mahājanas	brahmin residents of the entire village ; all the members of the village assembly

mahā maṇḍalēsvara	a feudatory ruler or governor
maṇḍala	an administrative unit
maṇḍalika	a feudatory
maṇḍapa or *mukhamaṇḍapa*	frontal porch of a temple
maṭha	a Hindu religious establishment
mukuṭa	a crown, cap
muṇḍamāla	a chain of skulls
naṭṭavulu	dancing girls attached to the temples
navagṛaha	the nine planets
padmāsana	a sitting posture with crossed legs ; the left hand rests on thigh and the other is held up
pāgas	segments produced upon face of temple by producing part of it to a more forward plane
pañchamahāśabdas	five great sounds
pañjara	representing a *nāsika* supported by pilastered frame-work at the lower levels of the *tala*
paraśu	an axe
parichāraka	an attendant
pāśa	noose
pīṭha	pedestal
prabhāmaṇḍala	halo round the head
pradhāni	minister
prākāra	enclosure wall ; compound wall
praṇāla	water-chute made for discharge of *abhishēka* water from *garbhagṛiha*
praśasti	a panegyric formula usually written in favour of a patron
puṭṭis	grain measure
rathāyukta	name given to the early type of *rēkha* temple
raṭṭaḍikaṃ	an administrative division

raṭṭōḍis	chiefs of *raṭṭaḍikam*
rēkha	typical Orissan temple tower
rēkha-deul	particular order of a temple
ṛishis	sages
sāla	rectangular on plan, and is similar is usage to *kūṭa*
sālōbhogamu	endowment of land for the maintenance of rest-houses and choultries
samabhaṅga	even bend, an erect stance with the weight of the body evenly distributed
samastāya	a tax on land
sandhivigrahi	minister of war and peace
sāni	a dancing girl attached to a temple
śaṅkha	conch
Saptamātṛikas	seven mother goddesses
satram	a rest-house, a choultry
śikhara	tower of a temple
Śilpaśāstras	Hindu texts on art, architecture and iconography
Sthānāpati	temple superintendent
tirumañjanam	the holy bath given to the image of the deity
tiruvārāyana	the sacred ritual
tōraṇa	arch, ornamental device, used either in relief or in free standing manner
trikūṭa	a type of temple plan
tripaṭṭa kumuda	segment of octagon
triratha	the three graduated projections of a temple plan in the northern usage
triśākha	triple jambed doorway
triśūla	trident
tuṇinēla	wet land
udarabandha	a band tied over the belly

upāna	sub-plinth
upapīṭha	an optional part of the plinth below the *adhishṭhana* proper
upavīta	upper garment
ūr	assembly of a village, a village
utkuṭikāsana	a sitting posture, in which one sits with heels kept close to the bottom
vaṁśa	lineage
varada mudra	formal hand gesture of granting a wish
veṇḍāya	tax on land
vishaya	an administrative division
vṛitti	a share in the gifted land, a share in the consecrated food
vyakhyāna mudra	formal hand-gesture of preaching
vyāla	a mythical composite animal of leonine form
yajñōpavīta	sacred thread across the shoulder
yōgapaṭṭa	a band of cloth tied around the upraised knees of meditating figures seated in a cross-legged position.

SELECT BIBLIOGRAPHY

Epigraphical Sources:

Annual Reports on South Indian Epigraphy, Madras, 1887-1945.

Annual Reports on Indian Epigraphy.

Annual Reports on Epigraphy, 1967, 1977.

Annual Reports of the Mysore Archaeological Department, *Bangalore*, 1906-39; Mysore and Hyderabad, 1965.

A Topographical List of the Inscriptions in the Madras Presidency, 3 volumes, Ed. by Ranghacharya, V., (Madras, 1919).

Copper Plate Inscriptions in the Hyderabad Museum, Vol. I, N. Ramesan (Ed.), 1962.

Copper Plate Inscriptions of Andhra Pradesh State Museum, Vol. II by Ramesan, N. (Hyderabad, 1970).

Early Telugu Inscriptions Upto 1100 A.D. by Radhakrishna, B., Hyderabad, 1971.

Epigraphia Andhrica.

Epigraphia Carnatica.

Epigraphia Indica.

Hyderabad Archaeological Series.

Indian Antiquary.

Inscriptional Glossary of Andhra Pradesh, Iswar Dutt, K., Hyderabad, 1967.

Inscriptions of Andhra Dynasties—M. Rama Rao.

Journal of Andhra Historical Research Society.

Journal of Andhra History and Culture.

Śāsana Padya Manjari (Ed.) J. Ramayya Pantulu.

Śāsana Saṁpuṭi (Telugu) by B.N. Sastry, Hyderabad, 1973.

Select Stone Inscriptions of Andhra Pradesh, Desai, P.B. (Ed.) (Hyderabad, 1962).

South Indian Inscriptions.

Temple Inscriptions of Andhra Pradesh, Srikakulam District (Ed.) N. Ramesan and Mukunda Rao (Hyderabad, 1980).

The Journal of the Epigraphical Society of India.

The Historical Inscriptions of Southern India and Outlines of Political History (Ed.) Robert Sewell, Madras, 1932.

Other Works :

Acharya, Prasanna Kumar, *Indian Architecture According to Mānasāra-Śilpaśāstra*, Patna, rpt., 1985.

Agrawala, V.S., *Śiva-Mahādēva—The Great God, An Exposition of the Symbolism of Śiva*, Varanasi, 1966.

Aiyangar, S.K., *Hindu Administrative Institutions of Southern India*, Madras, 1932 ; *Historical Inscriptions of South India*, Madras, 1932.

Appadorai, A., *Economic Conditions of Southern India*, 2 Vols., Madras, 1936.

Arokiaswami, "The Inscriptional Term 'Mūvēndavēlān' ", *Journal of Indian History*, Vol. 34, 1956.

Aryan, K.C., *The Little Goddesses (Maitṛikas)*, Delhi, 1980 ; *Basis of Decorative Element in Indian Art*, Delhi, 1981.

Asher, Frederick and Gai, G.S. (Ed.) *Indian Epigraphy—Its Bearing on the History of Art*, Delhi, 1985.

Balasubrahmanyan, S.R., *Early Chōḷa Art*, Bombay, 1966.

Early Chōḷa Temples, Delhi, 1971.

Middle Chōḷa Temples, Delhi, 1975.

Later Chōḷa Temples, Madras, 1979.

Banerjea, J.N., *The Development of Hindu Iconography*, Delhi, 1974.

Basavaraja, K.R., *Administration Under the Chāḷukyas of Kalyāṇa*, Madras, 1983.

Baskaran, S.T., "The Saptamātrikas of Perukanchi", *Lalitkala*, 1956.

Bloch, Marc, *Feudal Society*, London, 1961.

Boner, Alice and Sarma, S.R., Ramachandrakaulacara, *Śilpa Prakāśa*, Leiden, 1966.

Bose, N.K., *Canons of Orissan Architecture*, Calcutta, 1932.

Brown, Percy, *Indian Architecture—Buddhist and Hindu Periods*, Bombay, 1959.

Chakravarthy, J. and Bhattacharya, D.C. (Ed.), *Aspects of Indian Art and Culture, S.K. Saraswati Commemoration Volume*, Calcutta, 1983.

Champaka Lakshmi, R., "Peasant State and Society in South India", Review Article, *Indian Economic and Social History, Review*, Vol. 18, Nos. 3 and 4, 1981.

"The Dravidian Style of Architecture : A Historical Perspective", *Indian Horizons*, Vol. 31, No. 2, 1982.

"Historiography of South India New Directions," Presidential Address,

Historiography Section, *South Indian History Congress*, Seventh Session, Madras, 1987.

Coulbourn, R. (Ed.), *Feudalism in History*, Princeton, 1956.

Dehejia, Vidya, *Early Stone Temples of Orissa*, Delhi, 1979.

Desai, Devangana, "Art under Feudalism in India (A.D. 500-1300)", *Indian Historical Review*, Vol. I, No. 1, March 1974.

"Relevance of Tantrism to Erotic Temple Sculpture" in *Madhu* (Ed.) by M.S. Nagaraja Rao, Delhi, 1981.

Devanathachari, N. (Ed.), *Śilparatnam*, Tanjore, 1961.

Dikshit, G.S., *Local Self Government in Medieval Karnataka*, Dharwar, 1964.

Eisenstadt, *The Political System of Empires*, New York, 1963 ; *Society, Culture and Urbanization*, New York, 1986.

Eschmann, A., Kulke, H. and Tripathi, G.C. (Ed.), *The Cult of Jagannath and the Regional Tradition of Orissa*, Delhi, 1978.

Firth, Raymond, *Symbols : Public and Private*, Ithaca, 1973.

Fox, Richard, G. (Ed.), *Realm and Region In Traditional India*, Delhi, 1977.

Frykenberg, R.E. (Ed.), *Land Control and Social Structure in Indian History*, Madison, 1969 ;

Studies of South India—An Anthology of Recent Research and Scholarship, Madras, 1985.

Ganguly, O.C., *Eastern Chāḷukyas*, Banaras, 1937.

Ganguly, O.C., *Kōṇārk*, Calcutta, 1956.

Getty, Alice, *A Monograph on the Elephant faced God*, Oxford, 1936.

Gopinatha Rao, T.A., *Elements of Hindu Iconography*, II Vols., Delhi, 1971 (reprinted).

Gupta, S.P. and K.S. Ramachandran (Ed.), *H.D. Sankalia—Aspects af Indian History and Archaeology*, Delhi, 1977.

Hall, Kenneth, R., *Trade and Statecraft in the Age of the Cōḷas*, Delhi, 1980.

"Peasant State and Society in Chōḷa Times : A View from the Tiruvidaimarudur Urban Complex", *Indian Economic and Social History Review*, Vol. XVIII, Nos. 3 and 4, 1981.

Hall, Kenneth, R. and George W. Spencer, "The Economy of Kanchipuram—A Sacred Centre in Early South India, *Journal of Urban History*, Vol. 6, No. 2, February, 1980.

Hanumantha Rao, B.S.L., *Religion in Andhra*, Guntur, 1973.

Heitzman, James, E., *Gifts of Power : Temples, Politics and Economy in Medieval South India*, Unpublished Ph. D. Dissertation, University of Pennsylvania, 1985.

Ismail, K., *Karnataka Temples—Their Role in Socio-Economic Life*, Delhi, 1984.

Jha, D.N., *Studies in Early Indian Economic History*, Delhi, 1980.

Presidential Address, Ancient India Section, *Indian History Congress*, Fortieth Session, Waltair, 1979.

"Temples and Merchants in South India A.D. 900-1300," in *Studies in Early Indian Economy*, Delhi, 1980.

Kamesvar Rao, V., *The Lepakshi Temple*, Tirupati, 1982.

Kane, P.V., *History of the Dharmaśāstras*, 4 Vols.. Bombay, 1904.

Karashima, Noboru, *South Indian History and Society—Studies from Inscriptions A.D. 850-1800*, Delhi, 1984.

Karashima, N. and Sitaraman, B., "Revenue Terms in Chōḷa Inscriptions," *Journal of Asian and African Studies* (Tokyo), No. 5, 1972.

Karashima, N., Subbarayalu, Y. and Matsui, T., *A Concordance of the Names in the Chōḷa Inscriptions*, Madurai, 1978.

Kennedy, Richard, S., "The King in Early South India, As Chieftain and Emperor, "*The Indian Historical Review*, 3.1 (1976).

Kramrisch, S., *The Hindu Temple*, II Vols., Calcutta, 1946.

Krishnan, K.G., *Studies in South Indian Epigraphy*, Madras, 1981.

Krishna Kumari, M., *The Rule of the Chāḷukya Chōḷas in Āndhradēśa*, Delhi, 1985.

Krishna Rao, B.V., *A History of the Early Dynasties of Āndhradēśa*, Madras, 1942.

The History of the Eastern Chāḷukyas of Vēngī, Hyderabad, 1973.

Kulke, Herman, "Fragmentation and Segmentation versus Integration ? Reflections on the Concepts of Indian Feudalism and the Segmentary State in Indian History," *Studies in History*, Vol. IV, No. 2, July—December, 1982.

Lal, Kanwar, *Temples and Sculptures of Bhubanesvar*, Delhi, 1976.

Leela Shantakumari, S., *History of the Agraharas-Karnataka, 400-1300*, Madras, 1986.

Ludden, David, *Peasant History in South India*, Princeton, 1985.

Madhusudan Reddy, K., *Theory and Practice of Government in Medieval Andhradesa (1000-1400 A.D.)*, Unpublished Thesis, Osmania University, Hyderabad, 1973.

Mahajan, Malati, *Development of Material Culture In India*, Delhi, 1986.

Mahalingam, T.V., *South Indian Polity*, Madras, 1955. *Studies in the South Indian Temple Complex*, Dharwar, 1970.

Mangalam, S.J., *Historical Geography and Toponomy of Andhra Pradesh*, Delhi, 1986.

Masthanaiah B., *Temples of Mukhalingam*, Delhi, 1975.

Meister, Michael, W. (Ed.), *Encyclopaedia of Indian Temple Architecture : South India—Lower Drāviḍadēśa* (200 B.C. to 1324 A.D.), Delhi, 1983.

Mitchell, George, *The Hindu Temple*, Delhi, 1977.

Mitchiner, John E., *Traditions of the Seven Ṛisis*, Delhi, 1982.

Mukhia, Harbans, "Was There Feudalism in Indian History ?" *The Journal of Peasant Studies*, Vol. 8, No. 3, 1981.

Nagaraju, M.S. (Ed.), *Kusumānjali : New Interpretations in Art and Epigraphy*, Delhi, 1986.

Nagasvami, R., "South Indian Temple as Employer," *Indian Economic and Social History Review*, No. 4, 1965.

Nageswar Rao, S., *Temples of Bikkavolu* (Thesis unpublished), Andhra University, Waltair, 1982.

Nandi, R.N., "Land Grant, Colonization and Food Production (600-1000 A.D.)," *Proceedings of Indian History Congress*, 1970, Varanasi.

Nandi, R.N., "Client, Ritual and Conflict in Early Brahmanical Order," *The Indian Historical Review*, Vol. VI, Nos. I & II.

"Origin and Nature of Śaivite Monasteries" in *Indian Society : Historical Probings*, Delhi, 1974.

"Feudalisation of the State in Medieval South India," in *Social Science Probings*, Vol. I No. 1.

Narasimhamurthy, A.V., "Regional Bias in South Indian History," in Devahuti (Ed.), *Bias in Indian Historiography*, Delhi, 1980.

Narasimha Rao, R., *Corporate Life in Medieval Andhradesa*, Secunderabad, 1967.

Narayanan, M.G.S., *Reinterpretations in South Indian History*, Trivandrum, 1977.

Narayanan, M.G.S. and Keshavan, Veluthat, "Bhakti Movement in South India" in S.C. Malik (Ed.), *Indian Movements : Some Aspects of Dissent, Protest and Reform*, Simla, 1978.

Narayanan, M.G.S., "Socio-Economic History—New Trends—A Case Study of the Chōḷa Times," *Proceedings of South Indian History Congress*, Mysore, 1985.

Nicholas B. Dirks, "Political Authority and Structural Change in Early South Indian History," *The Indian Economic and Social History Review*, 3.2 (1976).

Panigrahi, K.C., *Archaeological Remains at Bhubaneswar*, Calcutta, 1961.

Pathy, T.V. "A Rare Sculpture of Śarabhēśamūrti or Simhaghna-mūrti," *Indian History Congress*, Proceedings of the Fortieth Session, Waltair, 1979.

Pramod Chandra (Ed.), *Studies in Indian Temple Architecture*. New Delhi., 1975.

Rajendra Prasad, B., *Temple Sculptures of Andhra Pradesh, Archaeological Series*, No. 50, Hyderabad, 1978.

Art of South India—Andhra Pradesh, Delhi, 1980.

Ramachandra Rao, C.V., *Administration and Society in Medieval Andhra Under the Later Eastern Gāṅgas and the Sūryavaṁśi Gajapatis*, Nellore, 1976.

Ramachandramurty, S.S., *A Study of Telugu Place Names*, Delhi, 1985.

Raman, K.V., "Folk Themes in Sculptures," in *Journal of Indian History*, Vol. L, 1972.

Śrīvaradarajasvāmy Temple—Kāñchī, New Delhi, 1975.
Raman, K.V., K.G. Krishnan *et al.* (Ed.), *Śrinidhi—Perspectives in Indian Archaeology, Art and Culture*, Madras, 1983.
Rama Rao, *Śaivite Deities of Āndhradēśa*, Tirupati, 1966.
Eastern Chāḷukyan Temples in Āndhradēśa, Hyderabad, 1964.
Ramaswamy, N.S., *Amarāvati : The Art and History of the Stūpa and the Temple*, Hyderabad, 1975.
Ray, Amita, *Life and Art of Early Āndhradēśa*, Delhi, 1983.
Raychaudhuri, Tapan and Irfan Habib, *The Cambridge Economic History of India, Vol. I, C. 1200—C. 1750*, Cambridge, 1982.
Sampath, M.D., *Chittoor Through the Ages*, Delhi, 1979.
Sanjay Subrahmanyam, "Aspects of State Formation in South-East Asia, A.D. 1500-1650," in *Indian Economic and Social History Review*, 23, 4, 1986.
Sarma, B.N., *Iconography of Sadāśiva*, Delhi 1976.
Sarma, I.K., *Development of Early Śaiva Art and Architecture*, Delhi, 1982.
Sastri, H.K., *South Indian Images of Gods and Goddesses*, Delhi, 1974.
Sastri, K.A.N., *The Cōḷas* (2nd edn. rev.), Madras, 1955.
A History of South India, Bombay, 1966.
Sastry, P.V.P., *The Kākatīyas of Warangal*, Hyderabad, 1978.
Śrēśailam, Its History and Cult, Hyderabad, 1982.
Satyanarayana, K., *A Study of History and Culture of Andhras*, II Vols., Delhi, 1975.
Seshagiri Rao, Ch. (Ed.), *Telugu Samskriti*, Vol. I (2nd edition, revised), 1983.
Sethuraman, N., *The Chōḷas : Mathematics Reconstruct the Chronology*, Kumbhakonam, 1977.
Medieval Pāṇḍyas (A.D. 1000-1200), Kumbhakonam, 1980.
Shanmugam, P., *Revenue System Under the Chōḷas (850-1279 A.D.)*, Unpublished Ph.D. thesis, Madras University, 1977.
Sharma, B.N., *Iconography of Sadāśiva*, New Delhi, 1976.
Sharma, R.K. (Ed.), *Indian Archaeology—New Perspectives*, Delhi, 1982.
Sharma, R.S., *Indian Feudalism A.D. 300-1200*, Delhi, 1980.
Sharma, R.S. and Jha (Ed.), *Indian Society : Historical Probings*, Delhi, 1974.
Shulman, David D., *Tamil Temple Myths: Sacrifice and Divine Marriage in the South Indian Śaiva Tradition*, Princeton, 1980.
The King and the Clown in South Indian Myth and Poetry, Princeton, 1985.
Sinha, Kanchan, *Kārttikēya in Indian Art and Sculpture*, Delhi, 1979.
Singh, I.P., Bhasin, *Anthropometry*, Delhi, 1968.
Sircar, D.C., *Studies in the Religious Life of Ancient and Medieval India*, Calcutta, 1971.

Studies in the Political and Administrative Systems in Ancient and Medieval India, Delhi, 1974.

Sister M. Liceria, A.C., "Emergence of Brahmanas as Landed Intermediaries In Karnataka c. A.D. 1000-1300," *The Indian Historical Review*, Vol. I, 1974.

Sivaramamurti, C., "Parallels and Opposites in Indian Iconography," *Journal of Asiatic Society*, letters, Vol. XXI, No. 2, 1955.

Sivaramamurti, C., *The Eastern Chāḷukyan Sculpture*, Madras, 1960.

Śatarudrīya : Vibhūti of Śiva's Iconography, New Delhi, 1976.

Ṛiṣis in Art and Literature, Delhi, 1981.

Nataraja in Art, Thought and Literature, Delhi, 1974.

Early Andhra Art and Iconography, Mallampalli Somasekhara Sarma Memorial Lectures, Hyderabad, 1979.

Expressive Quality of Literary Flavour in Art, Dharwar, 1974.

"Geographical and Chronological Factors in Indian Iconography, *Ancient India*, Vol. XI.

Śrī Lakshmī in Indian Art and Thought, Delhi, 1982.

Smith, Bardwell, L. (Ed.), *Essays on Gupta Culture*, Delhi, 1983.

Soma Reddy, R., *Hindu and Muslim Religious Institutions of Āndhradēśa (A.D. 1300-1600)*, Madras, 1984.

Somasekhara Sarma, M., *History of the Reḍḍy Kingdoms*, c 1325 to 1448 A.D., Waltair, 1948.

Somasundara Rao, C., "Konidena Inscription of Anna-mantri," *Svasti Śrī, Dr. Ch. Chhabra Felicitation Volume*, Delhi, 1984.

Soundara Rajan, K.V., *Architecture of the Early Hindu Temples of Andhra Pradesh*, Andhra Pradesh Government Archaeological Series, No. 21, Hyderabad, 1965.

Early Kaliṅga Art & Architecture, Delhi, 1984.

Early Temple Architecture in Karnataka and its Ramifications, Dharwar, 1969.

Glimpses of Indian History and Culture, Vol. I, Delhi, 1981.

Glimpses of Indian Culture, Architecture, Art and Religion, Delhi, 1981.

Indian Temple Styles, the Personality of Hindu Architecture, Delhi, 1972.

Spencer, George W. (Ed.), *Temples, Kings and Peasants - Perceptions of South India's Past*, Madras, 1987.

"Temple Money Lending and Live-Stock Redistribution in Early Tanjore," *The Indian Economic and Social History Review*, Vol. 5, No. 3, 1968.

"Religious Networks and Royal Influence in Eleventh Century South India," *Journal of the Economic and Social History of the Orient*, XIII-1, 1969.

"Royal Initiative Under Rajaraja I," *Indian Economic and Social History Review*, Vol. 7, No. 3, 1970.

Spencer George, W. and Hall, Kenneth, R., "Toward an Analysis of Dynastic Hinterlands : The Imperial Chōḷas of 11th Century South India," *Asian Profile*, II-1, 1974.

Srinivasan, C.R., *Kāñchīpuram Through the Ages*, Delhi, 1979.

Stein, Burton, *All the Kings Māna, Papers on South Indian History*, Madras, 1984.

(ed.), *South Indian Temples—An Analytical Reconstruction*, Delhi, 1975.

(ed.), *Essays on South India*, Hawaii, 1975.

Peasant State and Society in Medieval South India, Delhi, 1980.

Subbarayalu, Y., *Political Geography of the Chōḷa Country*, Madras, 1973.

"Mandalam as a Political Geographical Unit in South India," *Proceedings of Indian History Congress*, Hyderabad, 1978.

"The Cola State," *Studies in History*, Vol. IV, No. 2, July-December, 1982.

Subrahmanya Aiyer, K.V., "Largest Provincial Organisation in Ancient India," *Quarterly Journal of the Mythic Society*, Vol. 45, and 46, 1954-55.

Subrahmanyam, R. (Ed.), *Sri Mallampalli Somasekhara Sarma Commemoration Volume, Journal of Andhra Historical Research Society*, XXXV, Hyderabad, 1976.

Subrahmanyam Reddy, *The Sculptural Wealth at Mallam, Nellore District*, Kavali, 1984.

Subrahmanya Sastry, K.S. (Ed.), *Kāśyapa Śilpa Śāstram*, Tanjore, 1960.

Sukla, D.N., *Vāstu Śāstra*, Vol. II, *Hindu Canons of Iconography and Painting*, Lucknow, 1958.

Sundaram, K., *Studies in Economic and Social Conditions in Medieval Andhra*, Machilipatnam, 1968.

The Simhachalam Temple, Waltair, 1984.

Suryanarayana, K., *History of the Minor Chāḷukyan Families in Medieval Āndhradēśa*, Delhi, 1986.

Tirumalai, R., *Studies in the History of Ancient Townships of Pudukkottai*, Madras, 1981.

Thapar, Romila, *Ancient Indian Social History—Some Interpretations*, Delhi, 1978.

Vaidehi Krishnamoorthy, A., *Social and Economic Conditions in Eastern Deccan*, Madras, 1970.

Vanamamalai, "Consolidation of Feudalism and Anti-feudal Struggles during Chōḷa Imperialist Rule," *Proceedings of Tamil Studies*.

"State and Religion in the Chōḷa Empire : Taxation for Thanjavur Temple's Music and Dance," *Social Scientist*, Vol. 3, No. 3, October, 1974.

Veluthat, Kesavan, "Royalty and Divinity : Legitimisation of Monarchical Power in South India," *Proceedings of Indian History Congress*, Hyderabad, 1978.

Venkata Raghottam, "Rājendra Chōḷa's Raid on Śrī Vijaya in A.D. 1025—Study of the Political and Economic Dimensions of the Plunder Dynamic in Eleventh Century—Tamilnadu," *Tamil Civilization*, Vol. I, No. 3, September 1983.

Venkata Rao, N., *Lives of Telugu Poets*, Madras, 1958.

Venkataramaniah, N., Thc Eastern Chāḷukyas of Vēṅgī, Madras, 1950.

Vijaya Ramaswamy, "Peasant State and Society in Mẹdieval South India," Review Article, *Studies in History*, Vol. IV, No. 2, July-December, 1982.

Wagner, Phillip, B., "The Problem of the Trikūṭa in the Architecture of Early Medieval Telangana, 11th-13th Century A.D.," paper presented to the Society for *South Indian Studies*, Tokyo, 1984.

Williams, Joanna, G., *Kaladarshana* : *American Studies in the Art of India*, New Delhi, 1981.

Yadava, B.N.S., *Society and Culture in Northern India in 12th Century A.D.*, Allahabad, 1973.

Yazaani, G. (Ed.), *The Early History of Deccan*, 2 Vols., Bombay, 1960.

INDEX

FIGURES AND PLATES

Fig: 1 – KĀMESWARA TEMPLE AT GALLAVALLI

BASE MOULDINGS

1" = 10"

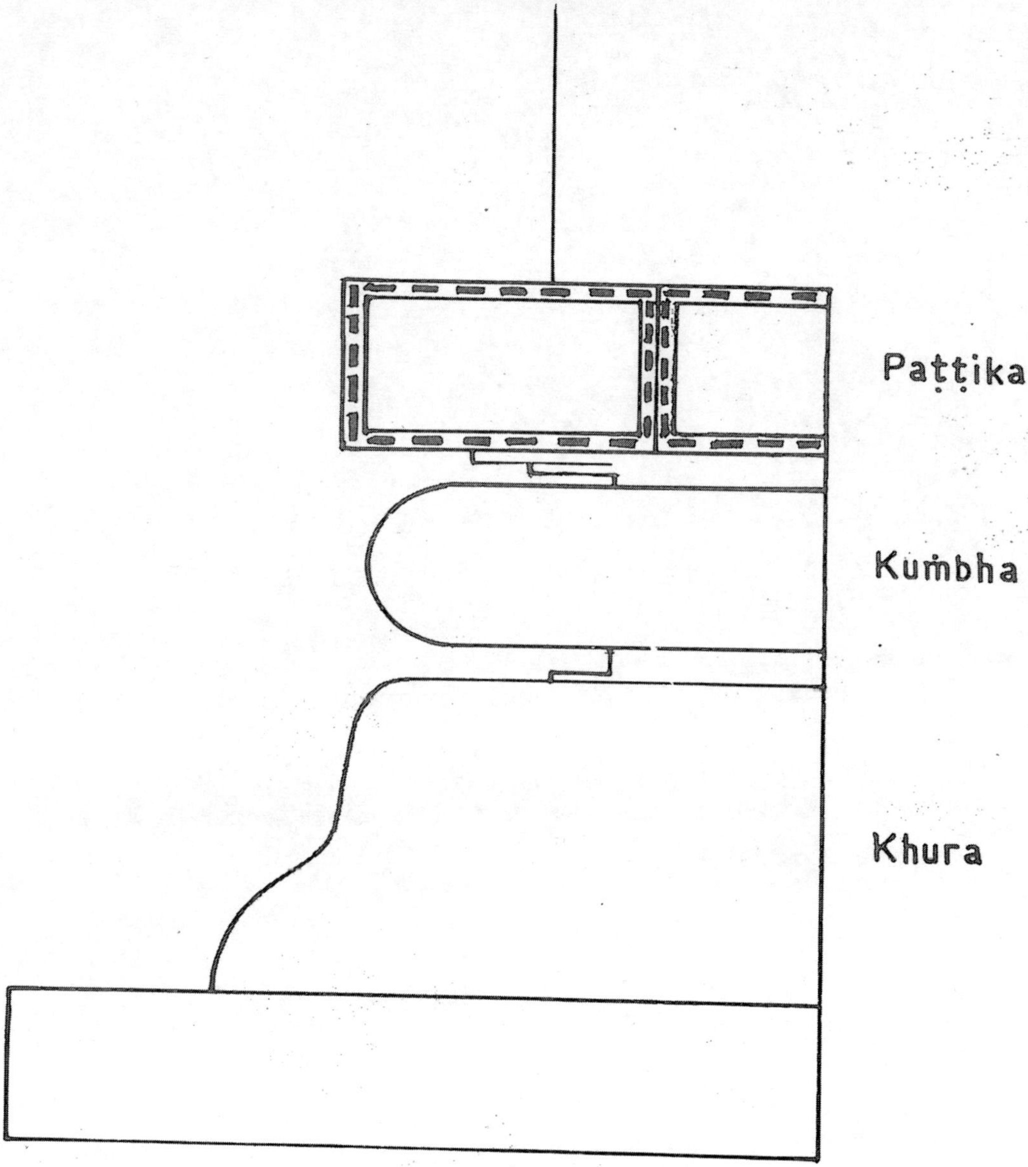

Fig. 2. Arjuna's Penance: Drākshāramā

1

2

3

4

5

6

9